LEARN
Your Way to
SUCCESS

HOW TO CUSTOMIZE YOUR
PROFESSIONAL LEARNING PLAN
TO ACCELERATE YOUR CAREER

DANIEL R. TOBIN

D1372018

New York Chicago San Francisco Lisbon London Madrid Mexico City
Milan New Delhi San Juan Seoul Singapore Sydney Toronto

1 2 3 4 5 6 7 8 9 10 QFR/QFR 1 6 5 4 3 2 1

ISBN 978-0-07-178225-8
MHID   0-07-178225-7

e-ISBN 978-0-07-178226-5
e-MHID   0-07-178226-5

McGraw-Hill products are available at special quantity discounts to use as premiums and sales promotions or for use in corporate training programs. To contact a representative, please e-mail us at bulksales@mcgraw-hill.com.

This book is printed on acid-free paper.

* * * *

For my mother, Eve Tobin,
who taught all her children the importance of learning

* * * *

CONTENTS

Introduction

WHAT DID YOU LEARN AT WORK TODAY?

> *Flexibility is the critical*
> *foundation for success.*
> *[Workers] need more than*
> *just mastery of subject matter,*
> *they need mastery of learning.*
> —Morris Weeks

You come to your job with a set of knowledge and skills learned from your education and your experience. Your employer may provide you with an initial period of training to get you up to speed and then offer you a week or more of training per year, but it is seldom sufficient to ensure that you succeed in your current job or to prepare you for the career path you choose to follow over the years. If you want to do well, if you want to excel in your current position—if you want to grow into higher-level positions over time—you cannot assume that your current level of knowledge and skills will be sufficient to take you through this journey. Nor can you rely on your employer to provide you with all the training you will need to succeed both today and tomorrow. You need to take responsibility for your own learning throughout your career.

Consciously or unconsciously, you learn every day. Starting with your first day on the job, you learn about company rules, the benefits the company provides, work schedules, which building entrance to use, whom you will be working for and with, and the requirements of the job that you were hired to do. However, your learning cannot stop there: you should be learning every single day.

> *In a world that is constantly changing, there is no one subject or set of subjects that will serve you for the foreseeable future, let alone for the rest of your life. The most important skill to acquire now is learning how to learn.*
>
> —John Naisbitt

Learn Your Way to Success is designed for every employee at every level, from the factory floor to the executive suite, from corporate headquarters to the most remote field location, from every line of business and every functional area. The goal of this book is to help you make your daily learning explicit so that you can consciously use it to improve your current job performance and your career possibilities. Too many people think of learning as an infrequent opportunity to attend a training program, take a college course, or go through an e-learning program. Whether you're aware of it or not, you are learning every day at work. In order to maximize your learning, you have to focus on the many opportunities you have every day and then on what you do with them—retention of learning greatly increases when you immediately use what you have learned.

Along with learning comes unlearning. The work methods that have served you well in the past may not be the optimal solution today or tomorrow. You need to question the assumptions under which you work—not just your own assumptions, but also the constraints under which you work. You need to learn to welcome new ideas and methods rather than to reject them offhand because the changes they may bring cause you to feel uncomfortable.

You need to ask questions, even if you fear that your question may expose your lack of knowledge on the subject under discussion; only by asking questions will you get the answers you need. You should develop your own personal learning agenda to ensure that you perform well in your work today and build your knowledge and skills for the opportunities that will come in the future.

How can you plan your personal learning agenda? How can you capture your learning and apply it to your work? How can you use the many learning resources available on the Internet to learn what you need to learn? How can you maximize your learning from attending a conference or trade show? How can working as a part of a team help you learn? How can you build a personal learning network that can help you learn throughout your career? How can you best keep track of what you have learned and what you want to learn?

This book is designed to answer all those questions while providing many practical tips and techniques to help you learn and apply that knowledge to your job to make a positive difference in your personal, group, and organizational performance results. My goal is to help you take advantage of the many learning opportunities that you have every day on the job, to help you make learning a conscious activity, to open your mind to new ideas and information, and to make you an active learner. This will help you maximize performance in your current job and prepare you for future opportunities.

Organization of this Book

Chapter 1, "Learning on the Job," discusses how to set your personal learning agenda and provides a methodology to work with your manager to do this. While the primary focus of this book is on informal learning, in Chapter 2 you will learn how to get maximum value from attending a company-sponsored training program or from taking an e-learning course. Working with your manager, you will learn how to identify your key learning objectives for taking training and develop a plan for how you will use what you learn on the job.

Oftentimes, people miss learning opportunities because they feel that they already know everything they need to know or that the person who is offering them an idea doesn't know as much as they do, so they reject the other person's ideas without really listening to them. In Chapter 3, "Recognizing Your Limits," we talk about having the humility to learn.

You cannot learn without thinking and mastering your thinking processes. Chapter 4, "Thinking Inside and Outside the Box," focuses on how you can develop and utilize both your critical and your creative thinking skills.

Many of the world's best ideas come from experimentation. In Chapter 5, we discuss how to learn from experimentation, or trial and error. Too many people look on any mistakes they make as failures—the key is to learn from your errors.

Perhaps the most common method of learning is asking questions. Chapter 6 deals with how to ask questions and encourages you to be a "smart dummy."

Most people, at some time in their careers, will be assigned to a work team. Chapter 7 defines all teams as "learning teams" and discusses how members must learn from one another or together learn something new. If learning is not taking place in this context, you don't have a team; you simply have a group of people who happen to work for the same manager.

The Internet is an amazing source of data and information on every subject you can imagine. Through the generosity of strangers who have posted huge amounts of material, you can find incredible learning resources and access them for free. Nevertheless, there are also drawbacks to using the Web: in most cases, the information you will find has not been verified, and there is so much information out there in cyberspace that you can be overwhelmed by the number of sites that come up in any search you undertake. Chapter 8 will help you sort through this maze and discover the many learning resources on the Web that have been made available by people largely unknown to you.

Many people, at various points in their careers, attend a conference or trade show. These events can provide great learning opportunities, but most people get only a small fraction of the learning value available from them. Chapter 9 provides guidance and worksheets to help you get maximum learning value from attending a conference or trade show.

There are many people that you will meet in your work life who can help you learn. In Chapter 10, you will learn how to build a personal learning network and how to get value from it.

Finally, the Appendix discusses how to set up and use a personal learning journal to keep track of what you have learned and want to learn. The personal learning journal is referred to throughout the book with ideas for what you should be writing in it and how you should follow up on your ideas and your learning.

Start Your Learning Journal Now!

It is my hope that this book will help you learn how to learn and, through your learning, succeed in both the job you hold today and the career you build for yourself in the future. Learning must be a continuous journey, and that journey should start immediately.

What did you learn at work today?

CHAPTER

LEARNING ON THE JOB:
SET YOUR PERSONAL LEARNING AGENDA

For many years, a great many companies could promise a new employee lifelong employment and a predictable career path. Today, very few, if any, companies can make that promise. Whether you plan to stay with your current employer or seek opportunities elsewhere, you cannot rely on your company to teach you everything you need to know or to create a career path for you—you must take responsibility for your own learning, your performance on the job, and the shaping of your career.

Even if your company has a formal training department and offers a catalog full of courses for employees, no one knows better than you what you need to learn and how it can be applied to your job to make a positive difference in your performance. While many companies have promised their employees one week or more of training per year, the reality is that when times get tough, the education budget is one of the first items to hit the chopping block. Even if you get the promised week of training each year, no matter how good it may be, it will not be sufficient to ensure your improved job performance and new career opportunities in your future with the company.

So you must take responsibility for your learning and for building your own career path. You must be in a continuous learning mode: learning every month, every week, every day. Without continuous learning, you may well find your job and your career at a dead end. In this chapter, you will learn how to identify your learning needs and set your personal learning agenda.

All Learning Is Self-Directed

When you go to a training program, read a book or article, or take in information from others in any form, someone has created the content based on what he believes you need to know. Sometimes he is right on the mark, and you find that all the information is relevant to you and serves your purpose. But more often, not everything in the program will feel pertinent to your job or your situation, so you need to pick and choose the relevant content within the topics and focus on it. In short, you need to direct your own learning.

Let's start with a simple model—the Four Stages of Learning—to see how this works.

Stage 1 of the model is data. Like most people, you probably find yourself inundated with data: every book or article you read; every e-mail, instant message, and tweet you receive. In fact, everything you take in through your senses is data, and you may often feel that you are drowning in it. Management guru Peter Drucker has said that when you take data and give it relevance and purpose, you get information; that is Stage 2 of

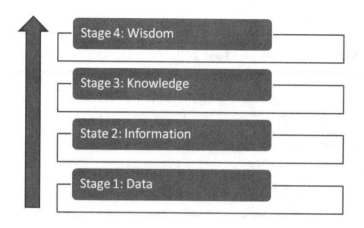

FIGURE 1-1: The Four Stages of Learning

the learning model. When someone creates a training program, writes a book or article, or teaches you something, she tries to filter all the data related to the topic and distill what she believes will be relevant and purposeful for you and other learners. But that person can never really know exactly what is needed by every individual who takes the course or reads what she is writing, so you have to do a great deal of filtering on your own. That is why you may be directed by your manager to take a course, but you must self-direct your own learning by focusing on the content that is most relevant and most purposeful to you.

When you take what you have learned and use it in your job, you are creating knowledge (Stage 3 of the model). You cannot say that you really know something until you have used it. For example, when you were growing up, you watched your parents and others drive a car. When you reached a certain age, you enrolled in a driver's education program and sat through classes in which an instructor told you what you needed to know to become a good driver. You may have used a driving simulator, where you had a steering wheel and foot pedals, and watched a video of roadways so that you could develop your skills in a safe environment. But you couldn't say that you knew how to drive until you got behind the wheel of a real car and practiced. Research has shown that if you do not quickly start to use what you have learned, whatever the source, you will rapidly lose any knowledge or skill you have acquired.

Stage 4 of the model is wisdom. Wisdom cannot be taught, but it can be developed through dialogue, demonstration, experience, intuition, and experimentation. As you gain experience in using your knowledge and skills, you may think of new ways to apply your learning and experience, and you may experiment to see what happens if you change one or more parameters. When you were learning to drive, you may have been taught what to do if your car

> *Learning is an active process. We learn by doing. Only knowledge that is used sticks in your mind.*
> —Dale Carnegie

hit an ice patch and started skidding sideways. If you live in an icy climate, you will gain experience in handling skids and build a sense of how much to correct the steering when your car is sliding, how much to use the antilock brake system, when to accelerate, and so forth. This is all wisdom built on experience, intuition, and experimentation.

The purpose of this book is to help you identify your learning needs, both for your current job and for the future, to recognize the many opportunities you have to learn as part of your everyday work, and to provide a guide to help you utilize those learning opportunities on a daily basis. In this first chapter, we focus on setting your personal learning agenda.

> *Learning is not compulsory—neither is survival.*
> —W. Edwards Deming

Your Manager: Your Partner in Learning

While you must take primary responsibility for your own learning, your manager is your most important partner in identifying your learning needs and helping you to find resources to fill them. How can your manager help in your journey?

- Your manager can help identify what you need to learn in order to improve your current job performance.
- Your manager can act as your teacher or coach for some of your learning needs and help you identify other resources.
- Your manager can guide you as you apply what you have learned to your job.
- Your manager can act as a guide to a career path within the company and tell you what you need to learn in order to prepare for it.
- Your manager can approve your application to take internal and external training programs.
- Your manager can give you developmental assignments that expand your role in your current job or prepare you for your next job.

Let's look at how you, working with your manager, can identify your baseline learning needs.

....

When I first became a manager, I was sent to a weeklong training workshop for new managers. In preparation for it, I was given a lengthy questionnaire listing many characteristics and tasks of a manager. For each of the more than 100 items, I was asked to score myself on two criteria: how I rated myself on each item, and how important I felt it was to my job as a manager. I also was instructed to give a copy of the questionnaire to my manager, who was also asked to rate me on each item and specify how important she felt the item was for a person in my job, and then to return the questionnaire to me in a sealed envelope. During the workshop, participants were asked to open the manager's envelope and compare their manager's assessment with their own. There were a number of surprises, both pleasant and unpleasant, that came from this exercise:

- *There were some items on which my rating was far above my manager's rating, for example, areas in which I thought I had greater knowledge or skill than my manager gave me credit for.*
- *On some items, my manager rated me higher than I did; that is, where she thought I was more capable or knowledgeable than I thought myself to be.*
- *There were some items that my manager felt were much more important for my job than I did.*

- *There were some items that I felt were much more important for my job than my manager did.*

This exercise led to a lot of discussion in the workshop and even more discussion with my manager when I returned to my office. It helped me to set my personal learning agenda, to set priorities for the skills I needed to develop, and to add some topics to my list that were things I didn't know that I didn't know.

Knowledge and Awareness

For each of us, there are things we know and things we don't know. We also have a level of awareness of our knowledge or lack of knowledge (see Table 1-1).

- In Quadrant I are the knowledge and skills that we know and use on a daily basis.

	Awareness	Lack of Awareness
Knowledge	Quadrant I: I know what I know	Quadrant II: I don't know what I know
Lack of Knowledge	Quadrant IV: I know what I don't know	Quadrant III: I don't know what I don't know

TABLE 1-1: The Knowledge-Awareness Matrix

- In Quadrant II are the knowledge and skills that we use, but that we are unaware of—our hidden assets.
- In Quadrant III are our blind spots—the things that we are unaware of, but that should be included in our learning agenda. This is where we need the most help from others in identifying our needs.
- In Quadrant IV is our presumed learning agenda—the things we know we don't know and therefore need to learn.

You have areas of knowledge and skill that fall into each of the four quadrants. Becoming aware of the contents of each quadrant can help you set your personal learning agenda. No matter how well you believe you are doing in your job, you need to be in a continuous learning mode in order to improve your current performance and prepare for the next steps in your career.

Using the Knowledge-Awareness Matrix

Let's look at each quadrant of the Knowledge-Awareness Matrix (Table 1-1) and examine how you can use it to identify your specific learning needs.

Quadrant I: I Know What I Know

These are the skills and knowledge of which you are cognizant. "I know how to create a spreadsheet program, how to use word processing software, how to write a performance review, how to troubleshoot a broken personal computer, how to use the company's e-mail system, how to write a marketing brochure, . . . "; these are the skills and knowledge that helped you get your current job. Your brain will also undoubtedly be full of other knowledge, and you may have other skills that are unrelated to your present position. Some of this extraneous knowledge and skills may have value in other parts of your life or at other times during your career (or in a trivia contest), but our focus here is on those skills and knowledge that are relevant to your current job.

Use Worksheet 1-1 (Job Related Knowledge and Skills Rating) to list your current job-related skills and knowledge and to rate yourself on each item that you list.

In listing your knowledge and skills, consider all the knowledge and skill attributes that enable you to do your job well. These may include the technical skills that you use every day to carry out your routine tasks, for example, entering data, using the company's e-mail and other systems, and telephone skills. But your list also needs to include the less apparent skills that enable you to work as part of a team, to relate to other staff members, to manage your time and your workload, to manage other people if that is part of your job description, to manage the parts of the business for which you are responsible, and so forth.

A good place to start in developing this list is the formal job description for your position, if one exists. While some companies have gone so far as to create a full competency profile for every job, most job descriptions are relatively sketchy and focus on key skills and knowledge for the position.

After you have rated yourself on each knowledge and skill area, you should also rate that area in terms of how important you feel it is to success in your current job. You will undoubtedly have some knowledge and skills on which you rate yourself highly but which have little to do with your work. It is important

Skill or Knowledge Category	Your Rating					Importance to Your Job			
	None	Basic	Average	Above Average	Mastery	None	Low	Medium	High
Knowing and Managing Yourself									
_____	1	2	3	4	5	0	1	2	3
_____	1	2	3	4	5	0	1	2	3
_____	1	2	3	4	5	0	1	2	3
_____	1	2	3	4	5	0	1	2	3
Knowing and Managing Others									
_____	1	2	3	4	5	0	1	2	3
_____	1	2	3	4	5	0	1	2	3
_____	1	2	3	4	5	0	1	2	3
_____	1	2	3	4	5	0	1	2	3
Knowing and Managing the Business									
_____	1	2	3	4	5	0	1	2	3
_____	1	2	3	4	5	0	1	2	3
_____	1	2	3	4	5	0	1	2	3
_____	1	2	3	4	5	0	1	2	3
_____	1	2	3	4	5	0	1	2	3
_____	1	2	3	4	5	0	1	2	3
_____	1	2	3	4	5	0	1	2	3

WORKSHEET 1-1: Job-Related Knowledge and Skills Ratings

that you recognize all your areas of strength; while some may seem irrelevant in your current job, they may become more important as you consider your next position and the shape of your career path.

You may also find ways of using some of your strengths to improve your job performance, even if they aren't part of your formal job description. For example, few job descriptions list a sense of humor as a requirement. But many people with a good sense of humor—who know when and how to use humor appropriately in their jobs—find that levity is a very effective tool for building morale, easing tense situations, and reducing conflict.

Categories of Competencies.

Whether or not you manage other people, there are three primary categories of competencies that can guide the list of knowledge and skills you create on Worksheet 1-1:

- Knowing and managing yourself
- Knowing and managing others
- Knowing and managing the business[1]

Knowing and Managing Yourself. In order to get your work done well and thrive in your workplace, you need to know and manage yourself, regardless of whether you manage others. Knowledge and skills in this category include such areas as self-awareness; self-confidence; time management; the ability to think critically, analytically, and creatively; having flexibility and resilience; and the ability to build trust with your coworkers and hold yourself accountable for your own actions.

11

You may have come to your current job with some of these skills already in place, while you may need to develop others. Depending on your present position, some of these competencies will be more important to your success than others; that's why the worksheet asks you to rate both your current knowledge or skill level and how crucial a particular area is to your job. In terms of your career path and the jobs you may want in the future, the competencies in the category of knowing and managing yourself may well be prerequisites for higher-level positions: if you cannot manage yourself, it is unlikely that your company will consider you as a good candidate to manage others.

Knowing and Managing Others. Competencies in this category enable you to work well with other people, whether as an individual contributor or as a manager at any level. Very few people work in total isolation, so you need to be able to work effectively with other people, be they colleagues, managers, customers, or suppliers. Competencies in this category include oral and written communications skills, relationship building, interpersonal skills, and, as a manager, performance management, delegation, and empowering and motivating employees.

It is important to recognize that a competency may be required for jobs at many levels of an organization, but that the nature of that competency may well change with the job level. For example, most employees in a company need to learn presentation skills, but the degree of skill required will vary with the level of the employee.

- As an individual contributor, you will need to be able to present your ideas to your manager and peers.
- If you are a sales representative, you will need to be able to make presentations to your customers.
- If you are a manager, you will need to be able to make presentations to your employees and also to your managers.
- As a senior manager, you will need to be able to present well to a larger group of your employees as well as to the company's executives and, perhaps, to the board of directors.
- As a C-level executive, you will need to be able to make presentations to all-employee meetings, to the board of directors, and perhaps to stockholders and the press.

So while your level of competence in making presentations may be sufficient at your current level in your company, you may need to learn more to qualify as a competent presenter at higher levels.

Knowing and Managing the Business. Competencies at this level again include some that are important for even individual contributors (such as knowing how to use company systems, problem-solving and decision-making skills, a results orientation, and the core functional and technical skills required to do your job) and some that are more relevant to managerial positions (managing and leading others, strategic thinking and planning, resource management, and so forth).

Again, start with your job description to identify the competencies in this category. If the description doesn't include a complete list, make a list of competencies and corresponding levels that you believe are necessary to succeed in your job. Once you have completed the list and rated yourself on each competency, specify how important you think every item is for your job.

Once you have completed Worksheet 1-1, it is important to review your ratings with your manager. You can ask your manager to complete the same worksheet and then compare your ratings with those given, or you can simply ask your manager to go through the worksheet with you and comment on the ratings you have given yourself. Your manager is your key partner in identifying your learning needs.

As in the story above, there will undoubtedly be some surprises when you do this review with your manager:

- There may be areas where your rating of your knowledge and skill is higher than your manager's. If this is the case, you should discuss with him whether (a) he doesn't know or recognize the level of knowledge and skill you possess, or (b) he feels that you need to improve in the area. A lesson to be learned here is that sometimes the level that you think is "good enough to get the job done" isn't good enough to meet the manager's or the company's standards. In the latter case, improvement in these knowledge and skill areas should become part of your personal learning agenda.

- There may be areas where the manager has rated you higher than you rated yourself. If this happens, you need to determine whether (a) this is an area where you have not recognized some knowledge or skill that you possess and that you should list in Quadrant II ("I don't know what I know") or (b) this is an area where the manager has presumed that you have greater knowledge or skill than you know you have. In the latter case, you should put the area on your personal learning agenda so that you can get up to the level that the manager expects.

- There may be areas of knowledge and skill that aren't on your list that your manager feels are important to your job. In this case, you need to examine each and determine whether it is something that you know or something that you need to put on your personal learning agenda.

- There may be areas of knowledge and skill that your manager feels are more important to your job than you do. For example, when people are promoted from individual contributor to manager, they often feel that they must keep their focus on the technical excellence that probably earned them the promotion in the first place. But your manager may feel that your personal technical excellence should now have a lower priority than managing the performance of those who work for you. Differences in how you and your manager perceive the significance of listed items are important points for discussion, so that you can know how to meet the expectations for your job.

Quadrant II: I Don't Know What I Know

In Quadrant II of the Knowledge-Awareness Matrix (Table 1-1) are those knowledge and skill areas of which you are unaware. Think of these as your hidden assets. You may discover some of them in your discussion of Worksheet 1-1 with your manager; these are the areas where she has rated you higher than you rated yourself. If there are some areas in this list that she feels are real assets for you, you may want to use them more consciously in your work, or you may want to develop them further. In the latter case, put them on your personal learning agenda.

Quadrant III: I Don't Know What I Don't Know

These are your blind spots: the knowledge and skills that are necessary to do your job well, but that you have never even thought of as things you needed to learn. As you work with your job description and as you discuss Worksheet 1-1 with your manager, you may discover knowledge and skill areas that you didn't know existed or that you didn't think were necessary in your job. As you discover each of these areas (and we all have some), put them on your personal learning agenda. But you also need to determine how important each area is to your success so that you can prioritize your learning agenda and focus first on the parts that are most critical to your success.

Quadrant IV: I Know What I Don't Know

This is the heart of your personal learning agenda. It includes those areas of knowledge and skill that you recognize as being necessary for your job and, at the same time, know that you need to develop from scratch or improve. Some of these items will come from your personal knowledge of your strengths and weaknesses, and others will come from the discussion of Worksheet 1-1 with your manager.

16

Summarizing Your Personal Learning Agenda and Setting Priorities

Once you have completed Worksheet 1-1; compared your list of skill and knowledge categories, your rating of yourself on each category, and how important you feel each is for your job role; and then reviewed your list and ratings with your manager, you will be ready to make a list of your learning needs and assign priorities to each identified category. Using Worksheet 1-2, "Prioritizing Your Learning Needs," list each skill and knowledge category that you and your manager identified, and write in your own rating and the rating that your manager gave you. For each line, then circle the importance of that knowledge and skill area as determined by your manager.

Now look at all the items your manager rated medium to high in importance: these are your highest priority. How much you need to learn in each area will depend on the ratings you gave yourself and those your manager gave you.

- Those items on which both you and your manager gave you low ratings (1 or 2) that your manager rated as being of high importance to your job should be your highest priority.
- If both you and your manager gave you above-average or master-level ratings (4 or 5) on an item, that means that you don't have a great learning need with respect to that item, and you should give it a lower priority.
- Items on which your manager gave you a lower rating than you gave yourself should be discussed with her to determine exactly what she thinks you still need to learn with regard to them.

Skill or Knowledge Category	Your Rating	Your Manager's Rating	Importance			
			(Manager's Rating)			
			None	Low	Medium	High
Knowing and Managing Yourself						
_____	_____	_____	0	1	2	3
_____	_____	_____	0	1	2	3
_____	_____	_____	0	1	2	3
_____	_____	_____	0	1	2	3
Knowing and Managing Others						
_____	_____	_____	0	1	2	3
_____	_____	_____	0	1	2	3
_____	_____	_____	0	1	2	3
Knowing and Managing the Business						
_____	_____	_____	0	1	2	3
_____	_____	_____	0	1	2	3
_____	_____	_____	0	1	2	3
_____	_____	_____	0	1	2	3
_____	_____	_____	0	1	2	3
_____	_____	_____	0	1	2	3
_____	_____	_____	0	1	2	3

WORKSHEET 1-2: Prioritizing Your Learning Needs

- Items on which your manager gave you a higher rating than you gave yourself are probably areas in which you have hidden assets—things that you didn't know you know. Examine each one see if you can become more conscious of those assets and start using them to your advantage, especially if your manager rated them as being of medium to high importance to your job.

It is important that you don't let the list of learning needs overwhelm you. Some competency models have as many as 100 or more competencies, but no one person will ever score perfectly on all of them. When an executive headhunter takes an assignment to fill a new senior-level position in a company, he often prepares a job specification that runs multiple pages and may contain dozens of competencies that describe the ideal candidate. But headhunters know that they will rarely find candidates who exactly match their specification and generally settle for candidates who meet 80 percent of the requirements. So once you have your list completed, discuss with your manager how to prioritize your learning needs, concentrating first on those that will improve your current job performance, and then on the ones that will prepare you for the next step in your chosen career path.

You Have Only Just Begun

Going through this exercise will get you off to a great start in setting your personal learning agenda: you will have identified a number of competencies required of you and prioritized your learning needs for each one. This is just the beginning of your learning adventure, however—you now have to determine where you will find the learning resources you need to meet your requirements. Today, you have a multitude of learning methods available.

For now, we will focus on learning methods that are sponsored or paid for by your employer. In later chapters, we will focus on learning methods you can use every day on the job as an integral part of your work. We'll start with these:

- Attending company-sponsored classroom-based or e-learning programs
- Attending external training from a wide variety of training vendors
- Taking college courses
- Attending a training program or an industry or professional conference sponsored by a professional or industry association
- Getting on-the-job training (OJT) and apprenticing
- Receiving coaching from your manager, a peer, or another subject-matter expert within the company
- Receiving coaching from an external coach
- Getting a mentor, inside or outside your company

Some of these learning methods require time off the job, such as days for attending a formal training program or a conference, while others can be integrated into your daily work. We will examine the more formal learning methods here; the more informal ways of learning as a part of your daily work will be the subject of subsequent chapters in this book.

Company-Sponsored Training Programs

Many companies have their own training groups that offer a wide variety of training programs on technical subjects, professional skills, and management and leadership development. Some of these programs will be instructor-led training that ranges from a half day to several days or even weeks, depending on the subject to be covered. Such programs are typically publicized to employees through posters, brochures, newsletters, e-mail announcements or postings on the company intranet. Enrollment in one of these programs requires your manager's approval. Your discussion with your manager, using the worksheets described in this chapter, will establish your need to attend one or more programs based on your identified learning needs. There are limits to the number of programs that most companies allow an employee to attend in a given year, however, not to mention that your manager may not want you to spend a huge amount of time away from your job.

Many companies also provide e-learning programs, designed in-house or purchased from an e-learning vendor, and make these programs available over the company intranet and, many times, from employees' home computers. While there is an ongoing debate over the effectiveness of e-learning in comparison with instructor-led training, e-learning can be very effective in transmitting knowledge, although skill development and behavioral training, as a rule, are better taught in a live classroom. You should examine the e-learning course catalog provided by your company to see if any of the offered courses match your specific learning needs. In Chapter 2, you will learn how to get the maximum value from internal and external training programs and from e-learning courses.

Programs from Training Vendors

In most metropolitan areas, you will find a variety of training vendors that offer a wide variety of training programs, ranging from how to use basic office software programs to communications skills to management and leadership skills. Searching for training providers on the Internet will help you locate local, regional, or national vendors that offer programs nearby. While the list of vendors will include both for-profit and nonprofit organizations, most of them charge substantial fees for their programs. Many companies will pay for their employees to attend an external program if there is a substantiated learning need that will benefit the company. But as with all company expenditures, there are limits on how much the company will spend for training an employee in a given year—and then only with the approval of the employee's manager.

As with most expenditures, it is up to the manager to ensure that the selected program will meet both the employee's and the employer's requirements. Most training vendors have customer service personnel who will answer questions about any given program, and if you cannot get the answers you need, you can always ask to speak with the course instructor before signing up.

Taking College Courses

Virtually every college and university in the world has a continuing education department that offers courses in the evening or weekends for working adults. While most colleges started by offering daytime courses for credit, many have also gone into the business of providing short-term noncredit training programs to compete with noncollegiate training vendors. Some colleges have also gotten into the business of producing and selling e-learning and distance-learning courses that students can access from their home or office. These colleges have counselors (rather than customer service personnel) to answer questions, and you can always ask to speak with the faculty before deciding to take a course or workshop.

Many companies have a tuition-assistance plan, where they pay part or all of an employee's costs to attend a college program. Check with your company's human resources department on your company's specific policies; some businesses will pay only for job-related courses, while others will pay only for courses that are degree-related. Tuition assistance in most companies is separate from the training function, and it has a separate budget and application process from those used for internal or external noncollegiate training programs.

Attending Training Programs or Conferences from Professional Associations

No matter what field you are in, there is probably a national or international professional association for that field. Many of these professional associations offer training programs to their members, along with annual conferences, local and regional meetings, journals and magazines, and Web-based libraries of white papers and other resources. Many companies will pay their employees' dues to belong to a professional association; some will also pay the fees associated with attending an association-sponsored training program, conference, or symposium. Many of these programs are open to people who are not members of the association, although there is generally a higher fee charged to nonmembers. How to optimize your learning from conferences and trade shows will be further explored in Chapter 9.

Getting On-the-Job Training and Apprenticing

Every job in every industry involves some OJT. Think back to your first days on any new job. During this initial period with a new employer, you learn such things as

- Where to report to work
- How to fill out a time sheet or otherwise record your attendance
- Working hours, including coffee and lunch breaks
- What benefits are provided and how to access them
- Who your manager is and with whom you will be working

In some industries, especially those with a unionized workforce, there may be a formal OJT program or apprenticeship program where, as a new employee, you spend time in a classroom as well as on the job learning a new trade. At other times, apprenticeship arrangements are much less formal, such as when your manager asks another employee to show you the ropes of the basic systems and methods you will use on the job.

Getting an Internal Coach

Often, while you may be very good at doing most tasks in your job, there may be one or even a few areas in which it would be in your best interests to improve your knowledge and skills. You probably don't need to take a training program, because you already know most of what you need and the training program would require you to spend a day or more in attendance just to get one or two hours of instruction in your area of focus. This is an ideal situation to get some coaching from your manager, from a peer who has already mastered the areas that you need to learn, or from another company employee who is a subject-matter expert in those areas.

My manager had asked me to prepare a report and a presentation for her on program data that I had been collecting over time and had in a spreadsheet program. While it was relatively easy for me to write the report, I did not know how to display the data in the spreadsheet program's elegant table formats. I didn't have time to go take a course, and a course would have repeated a lot that I already knew about entering data into the program.

I had seen reports generated by Jeff, one of my colleagues, and I knew that he was a master at producing the types of tables I needed. So I asked him if he could take the time to show me how the table functions worked. In 30 minutes, he was able to teach me what I needed to produce the tables for my report. It would have taken me hours to learn how to do this from the software manual. Having Jeff coach me saved me a lot of time and effort.

Getting an External Coach

Many companies hire external coaches to work with employees on particularly critical skills that they lack. This type of coaching typically involves regular meetings between the employee and the coach over a finite period. An external coach should have the opportunity to see the employee in action so that she can judge the kind and length of coaching needed and observe the worker's progress. Because of the expense involved in hiring an external coach, companies often will make this investment only for more senior employees, and the external coaching is often seen as a last-ditch effort to remedy a problem situation where the employee may be otherwise terminated.

Getting a Mentor

A mentor is a wise and trusted counselor who can provide you with advice on your company's culture, the industry in which you work, learning opportunities that may be available within the company, and advice on your career path. Some companies have formal mentoring programs, sometimes for new hires and other times for employees who have been designated as having high potential for future leadership roles in the company. You should check to see if your company has a mentoring program and what is required to become part of it.

Even if your company does not have a formal mentoring program, you may seek out your own mentor from within or outside the company, on a long- or short-term basis. The publisher of my first book told me that when he was a junior editor at a major book publisher, he was assigned a mentor:

a senior vice president who had been working for the company for several decades. They had lunch once a month for a year. "I learned more about the publishing industry and about how the company really worked during those 12 lunches than I could have on my own in 10 years," he told me.

Here's an example of how someone asked a senior company manager to be her mentor on a specific topic.

I was hired by a Fortune 500 company as a senior international human resources consultant. At my first performance review, my boss, a vice president in the company's performance resource group, told me that I excelled in every aspect of my job, but for me to move ahead in my career, I needed to learn to think more strategically.

I took her feedback seriously. Over the next year, I enlisted the help of Don, the company's senior vice president and director of corporate development and strategy, to teach me about strategic thinking. Every month or two, we met for lunch. I listened carefully to Don's stories about his own strategic moves, and he guided my decision making. What I learned helped me to think more strategically and, as a result, to advance in my career.

—Story contributed by Judith Lindenberger

In general, when you're looking for a mentor within your own company, that person should

- *Be at least two levels higher than you in the organization's hierarchy.* While it is possible for your direct manager to act as your mentor, her focus is more on your current job. You need your mentor to take a longer view of your career.
- *Be someone with many years of experience in the company and the industry.* You want your mentor to be able to impart wisdom from long years of experience.
- *Be someone with a broad enough view of the company to help you identify career paths and learning and development opportunities.* For example, the mentor might tell you that you should join a cross-functional task force to broaden your view of the company's business *and* have the power to either appoint you to such a group or influence your becoming part of that group.

The mentor-mentee relationship is built on trust. There are many ways that you can ruin such a relationship, including asking your mentor to second-guess your manager's decisions or using your mentoring sessions to complain about your manager. The relationship should be mutually supportive: you should think not just about how your mentor can help you, but also about how you can help your mentor. For example, a younger employee who is working with an older mentor may be able to help the mentor learn about social networking and how using tools such as Facebook and Twitter can help the company.[2]

We will discuss finding and using an external mentor in the chapter on building your personal learning network.

Chapter Summary

In this chapter, you have learned about the Four Stages of Learning and how you must take responsibility for your own learning throughout your career. You learned about the Knowledge-Awareness Matrix, how to use it to discover your learning needs, and how to partner with your manager to identify and prioritize those learning needs. You also learned how formal learning activities, usually sponsored or paid for by your company, can help you satisfy some of your learning needs.

In the next chapter, you will learn how to get maximum value from attending instructor-led training programs and taking e-learning courses. The remainder of the book will instruct you on how to identify and utilize informal methods to identify your learning needs and learn continuously from a wide variety of informal learning resources.

Notes

1. For a more complete listing of competencies in these categories, along with definitions and illustrative behaviors for each competency, see Daniel R. Tobin and Margaret S. Pettingell, *The AMA Guide to Management Development* (AMACOM, 2008). Please note that the AMA management competency model also includes competencies for individual contributors.
2. A good guide to finding and utilizing a mentor is *The Mentee's Guide: Making Mentoring Work for You* by Lois Zachary and Lory Fischler (Jossey-Bass, 2009).

TAKING TRAINING: HOW TO GET THE MAXIMUM BENEFIT FROM TRAINING

While the majority of this book focuses on the many informal learning opportunities you have as part of your daily work, there will be times when your manager requires you to attend a training program or take an e-learning course, and other times when you see a classroom-based or e-learning training program that you would like to attend. In this chapter, we'll talk about how to get maximum benefit from formal training programs, whether they take place in a classroom or via e-learning.

When Your Manager Sends You to a Training Program

You get an e-mail from your manager telling you about a training program that the company is offering and asking you to register and attend. Here are the steps you should take before, during, and after the program to ensure that you get the greatest benefit from it and that you meet your manager's expectations for your attendance.

Before the Training Program

You will get maximum benefit from the training program if you complete these five tasks before it begins:

1. Find the program description, objectives, and outline. Review those documents and think of what you can learn from the course that will help you in your current job, as well as in future ones.

2. Sit down with your manager before the program begins and have a discussion about what he expects you to learn in the program and how he would like you to use it in your work. You can also review the program outline with your manager, asking which parts of the course he feels are most important, so that you can focus on those key topics.

3. Based on your discussion with your manager, write down your key objectives for the training—what it is that you want to learn. List specific questions you want to make certain get answered in the class.

4. Arrange with your manager and your colleagues to cover your daily work responsibilities while you are at the training. Put an auto-response message on your e-mail and voice mail accounts that tells people that you will be out of the office and will get back to them when you return. The message should also include instructions on how to contact your manager or a colleague who will be covering for you if the sender cannot wait for your return.

5. Complete any prework required for the training program.

During the Training Program

You are taking this training for a specific purpose, and you will get more from it if you focus on the training for the program's duration, no matter whether it lasts a half day or multiple days. Think of the training as part of your work responsibilities, not as something that is taking you away from your work. To get the most from the training program, follow these steps:

1. Observe common courtesies. Shut off your cell phone, your laptop or tablet, and other devices so that you can focus on the training. If necessary, you can turn them back on during breaks. Arrive early the first day of the training so that you can get through any registration procedures, find a comfortable seat, introduce yourself to the instructor and your classmates, and get ready to learn. Observe start and stop times and break periods.

2. At the beginning of a training program, the trainer will often ask participants about their goals for attending the class. Take this opportunity to tell her about the objectives you developed after your precourse meeting with your manager. The trainer may say that your issues will be covered in the program, or she may say that she will make certain that you meet all your stated goals, even if some had not been included in the course outline. Either way, you are setting the expectation that all your personal objectives will be met.

3. Give your complete focus to the training presentations and activities. Don't work on other job-related or personal tasks during the class.

4. If you don't understand something or have a question to ask, raise your hand—don't be shy about asking for help! If you have a question and don't ask it, you won't get the answer. And if a question pops into your mind during the class, there are probably other people who have the same question. In some cases, the trainer may say that your question is beyond the scope of the class, but that you can see her during a break and she will try to answer it.

5. Take time to introduce yourself to your fellow participants, either before the class, during breaks, or during group exercises. In this way, you will start building your own network of contacts. The other participants are there for the same reasons you are, and you may be able to help one another reinforce what you've learned after the class.

6. Before you leave the program, ask the instructor for her contact information. Ask if you can send her questions that may arise as you try to apply what you have learned to your work. Also ask whether there are any reference manuals, books, or articles that will help you gain more knowledge about the subject, or if there is an online discussion forum on which you can ask questions and get answers from experienced people.

After the Class

You have completed the training program, but you have yet to begin your real work: to apply what you have learned to make a positive difference in your job performance. This requires that you follow up on the training program with your manager and that you follow through in applying your learning to your work.

1. Within a day or two of returning from the training program, hold a follow-up meeting with your manager to discuss what you have learned and whether this course met the objectives you had agreed upon. If you were not able to meet all your goals, discuss what you can do to reach them. Your manager may have other learning materials that he can give you. Alternatively, he may suggest that you partner with a colleague who is already knowledgeable on the topic, or he may offer to coach you himself.

2. Map out a plan with your manager for how you will apply your learning to your work, along with a schedule for one or more follow-up meetings where you can show your results to your manager and get his feedback and, if needed, additional coaching.

3. As you start applying your learning to your work, you will likely have questions about situations that weren't covered in the class, items you thought you understood in the class but are now somewhat foggy as you try them on in the real world, and so forth. Use the resources you have identified to get answers to your questions—contact the instructor, ask a knowledgeable colleague, or ask your manager. It is your responsibility to ask for the help you need to use what you have learned and to meet the original objectives that you agreed upon with your manager.

When You Ask Your Manager to Allow You to Attend a Training Program

There will be occasions when you see an announcement of a training program that you would like to attend and will need to get your manager's permission and his authorization for your company to pay for it. The steps to ensure that you and your company get the maximum benefit are very similar to those outlined in the first scenario, when your manager sends you to a course.

The difference when you are requesting to attend a training program is that you have to sell the idea to your manager. In the earlier case, the manager was asking you to attend training that he chose, so he already knew what benefits he expected you and the company to get from your attendance. In this case, you have to specify the benefits you expect and make the case for his approval. Here are some other points to keep in mind when you are initiating your request:

- If the training is on something that is brand new to the group or the company, you may need to provide additional information to your manager, beyond the course description and objectives—perhaps some articles about the topic or some testimonials from others who have taken the training and utilized it to improve their business results.

- If the training is on a new piece of equipment, software application, or work method, make certain that your manager understands any expenditures that will be required to apply the course content to your work. The training program may be relatively inexpensive, but if it requires your manager or the company to spend thousands of dollars on a new piece of equipment for you to use what you have learned, that has to be considered as part of the cost of your request.

- If the content of the training program is something with which your manager is not familiar, you may have to seek other people to help reinforce your learning after the training. See if there is someone else in the company who has already taken the course or is knowledgeable in the subject area who can act as your coach or as a learning resource. If there is no one like this inside the company, you may need to find an external coach, and this may add more cost to your training. Another alternative is to ask your manager to send at least one other person from the group to the training with you so that you can help and reinforce each other after the training. Tell your manager about whatever arrangements you make for this continuing reinforcement, so it is clear that you are serious about learning this content and about applying it to your work.

When Your Request Is Beyond the Scope of Your Job

There may be times when you want to attend a training program that is beyond the scope of your current job. Perhaps you are trying to expand your knowledge so that you can broaden your job responsibilities in your current role, or perhaps you aspire to another level of management and you want to get a head start on some skills you know you will need at that level. In these cases, you will need to broaden your discussion with your manager to include your career aspirations and ask his advice on whether the training you are requesting is the right next step. Remember that your chances of getting approval for this type of program will have a lot to do with how well you are performing in your job: if you have not mastered your current job responsibilities, your manager is certainly less likely to approve a training request so that you can expand beyond them.

Getting Maximum Benefit from an E-learning Program

Many companies provide employees with the opportunity to take e-learning programs. Some of them are generic in nature (how to use a word processing application or how to use a spreadsheet to create a project budget, for example) and may be part of a large library of e-learning courses that the company leases from an e-learning vendor. Other e-learning programs may be very specific to the company's products and services or to its systems and processes.

The movement away from instructor-led, classroom-based training to e-learning has been sparked by cost considerations—when employees take e-learning, there are no costs for travel to a training site, nor is there an investment in classroom facilities or instructional staff. We will not discuss here the pros and cons of e-learning versus instructor-led training.

The one criticism I will make of how many companies have implemented e-learning is the assumption they make that e-learning doesn't take time or concentrated effort. I have seen companies take a multiday instructor-led training program, convert it to an e-learning platform, and then assume that employees require no time to take the e-learning: either they can do it on their own time, or they can multitask, doing the e-learning with their other work.

If you want to benefit from e-learning, you must take it seriously and devote the same time and attention to it that you would if you were attending an instructor-led program. If your manager asks you to take an e-learning program, you should go through the same before, during, and after steps described earlier in this chapter with regard to instructor-led training programs.

Because most e-learning programs are taken at your desk or workstation, you are more likely to have interruptions and distractions than if you were away at a training facility. Here are some tips on how to get the most benefit from an e-learning program.

E-learning Tips

In order to get maximum benefit from an e-learning program, you need to follow many of the same steps that you used in taking a classroom-based, instructor-led training program:

- Prepare
- Focus
- Follow up
- Follow through

Prepare.

Whether you are watching a webcast or participating in some other form of e-learning, you should prepare in much the same way as you would for an instructor-led, classroom-based course. Here are the steps you should take:

- Hold the same precourse discussion with your manager that you would for a classroom course. Review the course outline and objectives with your manager, and ask which topics she feels you should focus on during the course, what she expects from you in terms of using what you will learn, and so forth.

- Check the computer operating system requirements for the e-learning program: is the desktop or laptop properly configured to display the e-learning course? It is better to discover this early, when you have time to remedy the situation, than at the start of the course, when you may suddenly discover that you cannot participate because you lack some piece of software.

- Find out if there are any discussion groups being set up to support the e-learning course, and register for them. If the instructor has said that questions can be sent to him via e-mail or by phone, get his e-mail address and phone number, and put them in your directory for easy access.

- Get a headset to use while taking the course so that any audio portion won't disturb people near you.

- Check the precourse requirements. If there is prework specified for the course, access the materials and do the prework before starting the course. See if there are any other documents that you need to download before the course begins, such as copies of slides or worksheets.

- Set aside the time you will need for the e-learning. Clear your calendar for those hours. See if you can forward your phone calls to a colleague while you are taking the e-learning. If that is not possible, find out how to forward phone calls directly to voice mail during these times. Are there any follow-up sessions being scheduled? If so, block out those times on your calendar as well.

Do Not Disturb

E-learning in Progress
Until _____

FIGURE 2-1: E-learning in Progress Sign

- Create a DO NOT DISTURB sign for your office door or the back of your chair to use while you are taking the e-learning program. (See Figure 2-1.)
- Find out if anyone else in your group is also taking the same e-learning course. If so, see if you can team up to help each other learn and apply your learning to your work afterward. If there are several people in your group taking the training, see if you can reserve a conference room and set up your system there so you can all focus on the e-learning program without the distractions you might have in your offices.

Focus.

You need to focus on your e-learning activities, just as if you were away from your office in a classroom. Here are some ways you can do this:

- Shut off your cell phone or PDA so that you aren't distracted by calls, instant messages, or tweets.

- Shut off the notifications for your e-mail account so that you aren't tempted to read e-mails while you are taking the course.

- Shut down all other applications running on your system so that they do not disturb you and so that you aren't tempted to multitask. Several research studies have shown that when you multitask, the quality of your work declines on all of those tasks.

- Display your STOP sign on your office door or the back of your chair.

- Use a headset so that you can focus on the e-learning and not be disturbed by extraneous sounds.

- Participate in all course activities. If the e-learning program is being conducted as a live webinar, answer any polls that the instructor conducts, and use the chat feature to ask questions when you have them. If the program is asynchronous, find out if a discussion group has been set up online to ask questions, and use it. If there is a follow-up session planned, use it to get answers to any questions you may have. Even if you don't have any questions, participate anyway, since the questions that others ask in the follow-up session may relate to things you should know but didn't occur to you to ask.

Follow Up.

Just as with a classroom program, you should review it with your manager within a day or two after you have completed an e-learning course:

- Open the discussion by saying, "Here are the objectives we agreed upon before I took the course, and here's how I did with respect to those objectives," and then give a report. If there are objectives you were not able to fulfill, ask your manager's advice on how to achieve those objectives.

- Map out a plan with your manager for how you will apply what you learned to your work, including goals, timelines, and what assistance you will need.

- Tell your manager about any resources available to you to help you with this application: the availability of the instructor, a course-focused discussion group, documentation, and other materials. Ask if your manager knows of other resources—materials, his own help, someone in your workplace who has already mastered the subject matter, or the availability of a subject-matter expert.

Follow Through.

Your e-learning course is complete and you have an application plan agreed upon with your manager, so now you need to follow through with that plan. Set up periodic meetings with him to report on your progress and to help you with any roadblocks you may encounter as you apply what you have learned.

Chapter Summary

In this chapter, the focus has been on how you can best utilize formal training programs, whether they are classroom-based programs or e-learning programs. In both cases, you need to set the stage with your manager, ask his advice on what parts of the training are most important for your work, and agree upon personal learning objectives for the training. When it comes time to attend the training, you need to complete any prework and then focus on the training for its duration, putting aside your normal job responsibilities for this period. After the training, you should follow up with your manager, agree upon a plan to apply what you have learned to your work, and then follow through on that plan, meeting periodically with your manager to report on progress.

Starting with the next chapter, the remainder of the book will deal with informal learning: the many ways in which you can discover your learning needs and satisfy those needs as part of your day-to-day job responsibilities.

RECOGNIZING YOUR LIMITS:
HAVE THE HUMILITY TO LEARN

> *It's what you learn*
> *after you know it all*
> *that counts.*
>
> —Harry Truman

I was planning a training program for sales reps and sales support personnel, and I wanted to have some engineers give part of the training. In this high-tech company, engineers were the elite, and they knew it. "You want us to talk to sales reps?" they asked with a sneer. "What value can there be for us in talking to sales reps?" Engineers typically referred to sales reps as "talking mouths," "bag carriers," and other derogatory terms.

I called in some chips that were owed me and got two engineers to participate in the training program. At the end *of it, they came to me, very excited. "You know, we actually learned something from those sales reps! Did you know that they actually talk with customers and that the reps know how they're using our products and what they'd like to see in the next generation of products we design?"*

Those engineers had no idea that they could learn something from employees as lowly, in their opinion, as sales reps. It was a revelation to them. And when I put on the next, similar program, I had many engineers volunteer to participate.

....

No one likes to be wrong or to admit that he doesn't know how to do something that is part of his job. You pride yourself on knowing your job and having the knowledge and skills to carry out your work, solve your own problems, and make your own decisions. You don't like to make mistakes, because making an error deflates your self-image and, worse, may lower others' opinions of you. Like the engineers in the example above, you don't want to hear ideas from people who you don't think are as smart as you and who don't have your knowledge, skills, and experience. You are the expert, and you don't like to have your expertise challenged. So, like most people, you tend to defend your actions, be reluctant to listen to other people's ideas, and blame errors on others or on circumstances beyond your control—and by doing all these things, you close yourself off from the many learning opportunities that arise in the course of every workday.

Keep an Open Mind

....

Jim had recently been promoted to head a business unit in which he had worked for more than 20 years. One of his first decisions was to reorganize the 3,000 employees into 15 self-managed work teams, all reporting to a small central staff. I met with him about six months after the reorganization.

"How's it going?" I asked.

"Really well," Jim responded.

"It is a very different way of working than the workers were used to for so many years," I said. "What has been the hardest part of this for you?"

"The hardest part is when some of the teams come to me with proposals to try something that I just know won't work. Maybe it's something that I tried years ago that didn't work. Or it may be something brand new that I just know in my gut won't work. But because I have empowered them to make their own decisions, I have to let them learn from their own mistakes," he told me.

"Any surprises?" I asked.

"Yes, a lot of them. I'd say that in about two-thirds of the cases, the things I couldn't make work or I just knew wouldn't work—well, they made them work. I thought that letting them fail would be a good lesson for them, but I'm the one who is really learning!"

....

47

Too many people who are promoted to management or leadership positions in companies believe that they need to know all the answers themselves. In fact, the people who are closest to a problem, closest to the operations, or closest to the customer are often the ones who can come up with the best solutions and ideas. It takes a large measure of humility for a leader to ask for help and to trust employees to find their own solutions and determine their own direction.

....

The company was a small metal-fabrication outfit. The great majority of its work came from making a single product for a single customer: machine guns for the U.S. Department of Defense. In the second year of a three-year contract, the company was producing 150 units per month, per its contract.

One Monday morning, the vice president of operations received a call from the Pentagon contracting officer. Could the company increase production to 200 or more units per month? The vice president asked for a few days to answer the question.

Studying the plant's operations, he found that there was one bottleneck in the production process that could prevent them from increasing production. This was a high-tech milling center where they took a block of metal and put it through a series of mills and drills to create the frame onto which all other components were attached. The milling center seemed to be working at capacity—150 units per month.

The vice president was loath to go to his CEO and ask for $500,000 to replicate the milling center, so he looked for another solution. He assembled a task force—consisting of his own two manufacturing engineers, two engineers from the manufacturers of the equipment in the milling center, and a consultant from the Pentagon—to examine the situation.

The task force met at the factory on Thursday morning. The vice president sent the staff of the milling center to another part of the factory for the morning while the task force closely examined the layout and functionality of the milling center. At the end of the day, they reported back: "We might be able to increase production to 175 or 180 units per month, but there is no way to reach 200 or more units. The company will have to replicate the milling center to increase production to that level." The vice president decided to sleep on the decision over the weekend before approaching the CEO.

On Friday morning, he was walking through the factory, and as he passed the milling center, the lead operator stopped him. "Hey, boss. What was going on yesterday? Who were all the big shots?" The VP told him about the request to increase production to 200 or more units per month.

"You know," the lead operator said, "I think we could do it—with some changes."

"Oh, really?" asked the VP, half not believing and half wanting to believe.

"Yes, we can do it," the operator said. Then he thought for a minute. "Last week I was down at that new sporting

goods store at the mall. They had these beautiful new base-ball jackets. Do you think, if we can get production up to the level you need, you might spring for new jackets for the five operators here, maybe with the company logo embroidered on the back?"

"I think I could handle that," said the VP.

Early Saturday morning, the five operators were in the factory. Three of them spent the day reconfiguring the layout of the work cell and fine-tuning each piece of equipment. The other two spent the day hunched over computers, rewriting the computer-numeric-control programs for all the machines. On Monday morning, the milling center was back up and running. And in the next 30 days, they produced 220 units.

....

It is not just managers who need the humility to learn from others; we all need to recognize that we do not, and never will, know everything we need to know. As a new hire to a group, you may feel that your college major that qualified you for an entry-level job in your chosen field should have prepared you for the job, and, therefore, you are reluctant to ask for assistance because you feel that you would be admitting that you don't know everything you feel you should know. So rather than exposing your ignorance or embarrassing yourself by asking a "dumb" question, you muddle through the situation, often not solving the problem you are facing or otherwise obtaining a suboptimal result from your work. You need to recognize that everyone faces problems she cannot solve alone, that everyone has things she needs to learn, and that you will never get the answers you need if you don't ask for help.

....

My first full-time job after college was at an educational publishing company. My job was to manage the reprinting of textbooks after the initial run. My responsibilities included reading the text to catch any errors that had slipped through and ordering new typeset sections to replace any paragraphs with errors in them before printing a second edition. In most cases, there was no information in the text or the editor's files about what typeface had been used. I was new. I was young. I was eager to seem competent. I didn't want anyone to know I had no experience differentiating one typeface from another. So I spent a whole morning examining the features of different fonts—the shape of the Q, the width of the W, the weight of the horizontal line in the capital A—trying to find a match so I could order three lines of replacement type for a photo caption. No luck. I ate my lunch at my desk in my cubicle, disconsolate. Then I heard my dad's voice in my head: "Being smart is not about knowing all the answers. It's about knowing what questions to ask and not being afraid to ask them."

I marched myself upstairs to the art department, introduced myself to a graphic designer, and asked, "How can I tell what font this is?" He gave me an on-the-spot tutorial on serif, sans serif, and display fonts. He explained the concepts of baseline, X-height, ascenders, descenders, picas, point sizes, kerning, tracking, leading, and more. He talked about the "personality" of type and how the choice of a typeface can affect page design. He was delighted by my interest, happy to share what he knew, and invited me to drop by any time I was stymied. I thanked him, and then he thanked me, saying, "Usually people just ask, 'What font is this?' and walk away."

I learned several lessons at work that day, the least important of which was that I needed the caption reset in Garamond.

—Story contributed by Elizabeth Black

Asking Your Manager for Help

Let's say that in the course of your daily work, you run into a situation that you don't know how to handle. You may have tried one or more ways to solve the problem, but they didn't resolve the situation. It doesn't matter what kind of challenge you face; it could be an imperfect product coming from the manufacturing process, a customer complaint you can't resolve, a line of programming code you can't get to work, or a medical procedure about which you are uncertain.

> *If you simply take up the attitude of defending a mistake, there will no hope of improvement.*
> —Winston Churchill

Your goal here should be not just to get the situation resolved, but also to learn how to solve similar problems in the future.

Don't be embarrassed. Don't be afraid to admit an error you have made. Don't fear that you will expose your ignorance.

Swallow your pride, and ask for help.

You go to your manager, explain the situation, and ask for help. You have two goals here: first, to get the problem resolved; second, to learn from the experience so that if you face similar problems in the future, you can handle them effectively yourself.

There are at least five ways that your manager can respond to you:

1. "Don't bother me. Figure it out yourself."
2. "Just leave it with me, and I'll take care of it."
3. "Here's what you need to do."
4. "Let me show you how to do that."
5. "What do you think you ought to do?"

Response #1 isn't very helpful. You return to your desk and keep trying. You may discover a solution, or you may not. If you do discover one, you have learned from experimentation. If you don't, you will have learned a lot of things that don't work, so you can avoid trying those solutions when you face similar problems in the future—but you haven't learned to solve the issue. Or you might just give up and let it go unresolved.

If you find yourself in this type of situation—when your manager tells you to go find the answer yourself—here are some things you can try. First, you can ask one or more of your colleagues who has more or different experience than you have if they can help. Perhaps they have faced a similar problem before and found a solution. If your company has a knowledge database, you can search that for an answer. If your business has a discussion forum, you can post your question there and see if someone else in the company can suggest a solution. Or you

53

can assume that your manager was having a bad day or was in the middle of something more urgent, and go back to ask your question when she has more time to give you. But don't just give up, because if you do, you won't have learned anything, and you may well face a similar problem or situation again in the future.

Some managers, especially those who were promoted to management because of their technical expertise, may find it easier and less time-consuming to give response #2: "Just leave it with me, and I'll take care of it." Or it may be that your manager is very busy and feels that it will be faster to just solve the problem than to teach you how to do it. In either case, say to your manager: "Thank you for the help. But could you explain to me how to deal with this in case it comes up again?" If your manager is too busy right at that moment to teach you, ask the question again when she has more time to give you.

Response #3, "Here's what you need to do," again saves the manager time. She gets your issue resolved without taking the time to teach you how to do it yourself. In some cases, this may be necessary. For example, if there is an emergency situation or a safety issue involved, her goal is to get the problem solved correctly and immediately, so she tells you what you must do. The problem is, you haven't learned much, and if you face a similar situation again in the future, you will still depend on your manager for an answer. What you should do here, either immediately or right after you have followed your manager's instructions, is to say: "Thank you for the solution. I'll get it implemented immediately. But could we arrange a time when you can explain to me how you diagnosed the problem and arrived at that fix? I'd like to learn to do this myself in the future."

Manager's Response to Your Request	Potential for Immediate Learning	Potential for Learning If You Follow-Up
"Don't bother me. Figure it out yourself!"	None	★
"Just leave it with me, and I'll take care of it."	None	★★
"Here's what you need to do."	★	★★★
"Let me show you how to do that."	★★★	★★★★
"What do you think you ought to do?"	★★★★	★★★★★

Table 3-1: Learning Potential from Asking Your Manager to Help You Solve a Problem

Response #4, "Let me show you how to do that," is a much better answer. Your manager is taking the time to teach you how to analyze and solve the problem. Because of her willingness to help you learn, make certain that you use the opportunity to ask any questions you have about analyzing similar issues and selecting the right resolution.

Response #5 signals that your manager is taking the time to coach you. She may feel that you already have the ability to find the answer but don't have enough confidence in your own abilities; she may not have a ready answer and wants to explore possibilities with you; or she may be trying to help you better analyze the situation through her questions. This, again, is a prime learning opportunity for you.

As shown in Table 3-1, the potential for your learning is different for each of these five types of response to your asking your manager to help you solve a problem. In every case, there will be a greater learning opportunity for you if you follow up with your manager as described above.

"If It Ain't Broke, Don't Fix It"

You have been doing your job the same way for a long time, and you have been getting the job done adequately. One day, a colleague, your manager, or one of your employees comes to you and suggests a different way of doing the work. This person may have read about some new method, or may have seen a demonstration at a conference, or may just have been experimenting with how he does his own work; no matter how he got the idea, he is now offering it as a way of improving productivity or saving money or improving quality.

What is your reaction to this suggestion? For many people, the first reaction is the old saw, "If it ain't broke, don't fix it." Your current methods are getting the job done within the parameters set by the company. If you try something new and it doesn't result in improvement, you will be worse off than you are currently because you won't be able to meet your individual or group goals. And even if it does work, learning new ways of working takes time and usually results in temporary decreases in productivity as you absorb the information and implement the methods, even if they improve your productivity in the longer term.

So what do you do in this situation? You get uncomfortable. You resist change. You may even take the suggestion of there being a better way to do your job as a personal affront, so you become defensive about your current work methods. You try to find ways of killing the new idea.

From Idea Killers ("Yes, but…") to Idea Starters ("Yes, and…")

You are sitting in a meeting with your colleagues and your manager. Someone offers a new idea. Your first thought is how to squelch the suggestion, so you respond with an "idea killer," such as

- That will never work here!

- We tried that years ago and it didn't work!

- That may have worked in another company, but it won't work here. We're different!

- We don't have time (or the budget) for that!

- Who asked you?

- The executives won't go for it!

- Since when are you the expert?

- It can't be done!

- Let's be realistic!

- That's a dumb idea!

....

The director of technical documentation attended an industry conference where he heard a speaker from another company describe how they had cut the time to produce documentation on a new product to half of what the director's business required. After the presentation, he asked the speaker if he could send someone to learn more about how they were able to achieve this. After getting the speaker's agreement, the director returned to his office and asked one of the managers who reported to him to make the trip.

After the manager spent two days visiting the other company, he returned with this report: "They use a better document development application than we have. They also get their technical writers involved with the product development team three months earlier in the design cycle than we do. Finally, their writers have taken a great workshop on writing documentation, which taught them some new and different methods that seem to cut down the amount of editing and rewriting needed to complete their documentation. Given these constraints, I'd say we are doing just fine the way we are."

....

This manager was afraid to change. He was afraid of learning things that would take him out of his comfort zone. He had three opportunities to recommend changes based on his findings from the other company, and he rejected each one. He visited the other company and discovered how the employees became more productive than his own, but he didn't learn from

58

the experience. He felt that his group's productivity was "good enough," that his discomfort with change was more important than the opportunity to improve, and, therefore, that he had no reason to challenge the status quo.

Alternatively, he might have been suffering from the not-invented-here syndrome, feeling that if he admitted that the other company had a better way of doing things, it meant that the people there were smarter than him. So he rejected the other company's processes, saying, "They're doing a great job over there. But you have to understand that we're different, and the processes that I've put in place for my group are perfect for our situation."

He also lost his job shortly after he gave his report. What could he have done with his findings from his visit to the other company to improve his group's productivity and to save his position? He could have extended his learning by suggesting

- Contacting the vendor to learn more about the software application the other company's technical documentation group was using: its functionality, cost, needed training, and so forth.
- Setting up a meeting with the product development team to discuss involving his technical writers with new products earlier in the development cycle.
- Attending or sending some of his direct reports to the training program the other company was using to see what new ideas were being presented, and then discussing how to use those ideas to improve his group's results.

When you stop an idea without giving it any consideration other than your own comfort level, you are blocking a key opportunity to learn and improve. If you miss too many of these opportunities, you will likely limit your chances of improving your own job performance and your career possibilities.

> *There is nothing permanent except change.*
> —Heraclitus

In this world, the rate of change is constantly increasing, and if you ignore or resist change, you will find yourself out-of-date and perhaps out of a job. Constant change requires constant learning, and when you reject suggested changes out of hand, you are blocking an important opportunity to learn and improve.

> *We now accept the fact that learning is a lifelong process of keeping abreast of change. And the most pressing task is to teach people how to learn.*
> —Peter Drucker

So instead of rejecting a new idea immediately, take the time to explore it and to learn from those who are presenting it. Instead of responding to an idea with an idea killer, respond with an "idea starter."

- Sounds interesting. Tell us more!
- This has potential!
- Whose support do you need? How can I help?
- How much time will it take to develop this further? What's the next step?

- What can we add to this idea to make it better? ("Yes, and ...")
- How would that work here?
- What do you see as the benefits to our group and to the company?
- What do you need us to do to make this happen?
- Where has this been done before? Can we set up a visit with that company to learn more?

Only by opening your mind to new ideas can you learn. With the rate of change and the rate of knowledge creation increasing constantly, if you view learning and change as challenges to your ego, or as too uncomfortable for you to consider, you limit your chances to develop and progress. Only by continuously learning and changing will you be able to improve your own, your group's, and your company's performance over time.

Chapter Summary

Most people have some level of ego invested in their jobs and are loath to expose areas where they need help or to admit that someone else's ideas or approaches may be better than their own. But if you never ask for help when you need it, and if you reject ideas or methods that you didn't generate yourself, you are closing yourself off from the possibility of learning from others and thus limiting your

Never become so much of an expert that you stop gaining expertise. View life as a continuous learning experience.

—Denis Waitley

61

opportunity to improve your own job performance and career options. So rather than acting on the impulse to reject others' ideas, listen to them and contribute to their development—you never know what you can learn. And if you run into a problem or a situation in which you aren't sure what to do, ask your manager for help and follow up with him to ensure that you not only learn how to solve the current problem, but also improve your problem resolution skills for when similar problems occur in the future, as they inevitably will.

Thinking Inside and Outside the Box: Utilize Critical and Creative Thinking

One of the most overused phrases in organizations today is, "Let's think outside the box." You probably have heard it, but you may not know its origin. It comes from an exercise using nine dots as shown in Figure 4-1.

The instructions for this exercise are to connect all nine dots using four straight lines without lifting your pencil or retracing any segment, so that each line starts from where the last one ends. If you have never seen this exercise, take a couple of minutes and try it before you continue to read.

The solution to the exercise is shown in Figure 4-2.

FIGURE 4-1: Connect the Dots

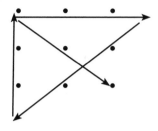

FIGURE 4-2: The Dots Connected

When most people see the square array dots, they assume that the dots form a box and that in drawing their four lines, they cannot move the pencil beyond the edges of the box. With this assumption in place, the puzzle cannot be solved—the solution requires that you move your pencil beyond the square: to think outside the box.

Working under Assumptions and Biases

We all have built-in biases and work under a set of assumptions. Biases come from how we were raised and our life experiences; assumptions are beliefs we have that we can't necessarily prove and that may or may not be correct. An example of a bias may be that you once purchased a product from a company and it worked poorly, so you now have a bias against buying anything from that company. An example of an assumption is that you may have heard that the company is tightening its fiscal controls, so you decide that you will never ask your manager to approve an increase in your project's budget because you believe that such requests will automatically be turned down.

A group manager had brought in a consultant. "I gave my group an assignment to develop a plan for a new product line," she told the consultant. "They have been at it for four months, and I have nothing from them at all—they keep stalling. I want to you to find out why they are stuck."

Several days later, after interviewing the group as a whole and as individual members, the consultant met with the group manager again. "So what's the problem?" she asked him.

"The problem is you," replied the consultant. "They have been working with a set of assumptions and constraints that you gave them last year. Every plan they have drafted, and which they believe to be reasonable, violates one or more of your constraints—such as no new hiring and no new plant or equipment, so they are loath to bring you their solution."

"Oh!" said the group manager. "Those constraints were cancelled four months ago. It's my fault for not letting them know. I'm glad to know that I am the problem here: me, I can fix!"

Critical Thinking

Many people are wary of the word *critical*, thinking that it implies criticism, meaning disapproval or censure. Critical thinking is based on a different definition of *criticism*—analytical thinking. The components of critical thinking include

1. Identifying and challenging assumptions
2. Challenging the importance of context

3. Imagining and exploring alternatives

4. Reflective skepticism[1]

Identifying and Challenging Assumptions

When people are stumped by the nine dots puzzle, they are most often working under the assumption that the nine dots form a box and that they are not allowed to draw their line segments outside its limits. Similarly, the consultant's report on why the team was at an impasse in developing the new product plan was that they were working under a set of constraints that they assumed were true.

Working under a set of assumptions will always limit your thinking and the number and kinds of alternatives you examine. How can you remove unnecessary constraints? The answer is that you need to identify the assumptions you have about a given situation and then examine them if you believe that they will lead to a suboptimal result.

• If you are given a new assignment, ask your manager what constraints there are on your solution.

• If you offer a solution to a problem and get the response, "It will never work here," ask why the objector feels this way. This will require the objector to specify the assumptions that resulted in the comment.

• If you are starting work on a team project, first ask the sponsor of the project to specify any limits he is imposing on the team's solution. Then, ask each team member what constraints they place on the team's work and determine if each is real or imagined. If a constraint is real, it will save the team from considering solutions that violate it; if a constraint is imagined (i.e., not really in play), it will open the team's range of possible solutions beyond that false limitation.

Challenging the Importance of Context

One of my first corporate training jobs was as a curriculum manager for a product line at a computer manufacturer. In conducting a needs analysis for the software specialists for whose training I was responsible, I identified a need to train them on a competitor's product strategy. The requirement arose because my company both competed with the other company and they also sold products that worked with the competitor's products. By training our specialists on the other company's product line, they would be better able to compete with it for sales and more easily sell our complementing products.

My proposal to develop this new program, based on solid data I collected through the needs assessment, was not approved. An internal development group did all course development in my company, and, I was told, it was company policy never to develop training on competitors' products. While I presented evidence of the learning need, the company had put this policy in place more than 20 years earlier and wasn't going to change it.

I had been working under the assumption that we would create training to respond to the real needs of the field personnel that we supported. What I discovered was that this policy was a real constraint on my planning.

You need to discover the context under which decisions are being made and, if necessary, to challenge that context with hard data and relevant information. If you have done your homework and believe that you are right, then you should challenge the constraints or find a way to work around them. In my real-world example, I found an external vendor who had a two-day training seminar on the competitor's products that would give my target audience the information they needed to compete. I then got my company's product manager to put together and present a third day of training on our products that complemented the competitor's. Using this strategy, I was able to get 300 people trained at a cost that was less than having our internal-development group develop a similar program. It was done within a few months of plan approval, while using the internal development group would have required a one-year lead time.

While doing background research and interviews for a case study on how a major manufacturer of telephone switches had used high-performance work strategies to cut the time to produce a large, expensive telephone switch from 10 weeks to less than 3 weeks, the company's vice president of employee relations asked me to include the union's shop steward in my schedule.

I asked the shop steward what the union's position was on the new program. "We're against it!" he stated loudly. When I asked why the union objected to the program, he told me: "They're cutting the work from 10 weeks to 3 weeks. The union's job is to preserve work for its members, and this will cut the amount of work available."

What the shop steward didn't understand was that the time savings came from eliminating bottlenecks where partially completed switches just queued up on the factory floor for days or weeks waiting for the next step in the manufacturing process. There was actually no work being lost—just waiting time between the various work processes. Unfortunately, the union didn't understand how this was working, and its position was that anything that shortened the time for manufacturing from start to finish was "stealing" work from union members.

Take the time to understand the context in which others are working, and if you believe the context to be incorrect, take steps to help people examine and understand that context. Sometimes, you may find that the position is so deeply ingrained that there is no way to change their thinking. In these cases, you will need to find a work-around: a way to accomplish what you feel is needed without changing the others' context.

> *If your employer starts upon a course you think will prove injurious, tell him so, protest, give your reasons, and stand to them unless convinced you are wrong.*
>
> —Andrew Carnegie

Imagining and Exploring Alternatives

We all develop our own ways of accomplishing our work. When we find a method that works for us, that enables us to meet the job requirements set by our manager, we then tend to defend our work methods: "If it ain't broke, don't fix it!" When you take this attitude toward your job, you lose many opportunities to improve your performance.

> When you consider something "ideal," you lose the opportunity to improve it.
> —Shoji Shiba

Why does this happen? Because most people do not want to make mistakes, and once they find something that works, they may not want to risk trying anything new because the new method may result in an error or in poorer job performance. But if you never explore alternative ways of accomplishing your work, you lose the opportunity for improvement. According to Peter B. Vaill, professor of management at Antioch University, "Learning is a willingness to let one's ability and attitude change in response to new ideas, information, and experiences."[2] So, if you close yourself off from new ideas, information, and experiences, you deny yourself the opportunity to learn, and therefore to improve your job performance. So how can you open yourself to new ideas and information? Here are a few ways:

- Talk with your colleagues who are doing the same or similar work. Ask them how they do their jobs and offer to explain your own work methods. If one of these people is doing the same work using different techniques, and getting better results, experiment with these alternatives to see if you can improve your own performance. Often, this does not require that you totally abandon your own work methods, but only that you slightly alter one part in order to get better results. Similarly, your colleagues may learn something new from you to improve their job performance.

- Read industry or technical journals and magazines in your industry or field to see what new or alternative ideas are being reported. If you see something that you believe could help improve your own or your group's productivity, experiment with it to see if it will work. If you are unwilling to take this type of risk on your own, give copies to your colleagues and your manager, and ask their opinion. Remember that in trying anything new, there is a learning curve—meaning that your initial productivity may decline while you absorb the new work techniques, but it will improve over time as you master them. Getting your manager's upfront agreement to the new methods can ensure that you are not penalized for any initial drop in productivity.

- Volunteer to be a part of any external benchmarking team that is visiting another company to see how it is doing work similar to your own. Similarly, if you have an opportunity to attend an industry conference or a trade show, keep your mind open to new ideas and information. You never know when you will find something that can help you improve your work.

- If you make a mistake, don't hide it or defend it. Instead, learn from it. Why did the error happen? How can you prevent similar errors in the future? As Winston Churchill once said, "If you simply take up the attitude of defending

71

a mistake, there will be no hope of improvement." And once you have learned from it, share your learning with others, so that they can avoid making the same error.

At one company, if an employee followed a logical path to solve a problem and ended up making an error, the employee's manager could pay the employee $50 to write up the experience and post it on the intranet. The point of this was not to embarrass the employee but to have the employee help others avoid a similar mistake. The value of saving one or more other employees from making the same error was almost always worth more than the $50 investment.

Sometimes, people are hesitant to reveal their "hidden agendas," or their assumptions are so deeply ingrained that they cannot easily identify them. Here's a way to help uncover hidden or unobvious assumptions and constraints. Let's say that your group is holding a brainstorming session to generate new ideas and alternatives on how to approach a new project. Once the initial brainstorming is completed and you have a list of ideas, ask each person in the group to vote for his or her favorite. Rather than just recording each vote, ask each person to state the reason for his vote.

- Someone may say, "I like Idea #4 because we can do it within the time frame for the project." This tells you that the person is concerned with a time constraint.

- Another person might say, "I like Idea #12 because it won't require any more people than we already have." This assumes that there is a constraint with regard to hiring new people.
- A third person might say, "I like Idea #7 because it won't require us to buy any more equipment." This assumes a constraint on the purchase of new equipment.

By identifying the reasons for the votes, you can uncover each person's assumptions about constraints and then test those assumptions to see whether they actually exist.

Reflective Skepticism

Being open to new ideas and alternatives does not require blind acceptance of every new idea. Stephen Brookfield defines reflective skepticism as "being wary of uncritically accepting an innovation, change, or new perspective simply because it is new," but, rather, having "a readiness to test the validity of claims made by others for any presumed givens, final solutions, and ultimate truths against one's own experience of the world."[2]

....

I have never liked the term best practice. It implies that there has been a scientific study of all alternative approaches and that, from this research, one practice has been proven to be the universal "best." In fact, what may be best for one company or one industry or one group may not be so for a different company, industry, or group that finds itself in different circumstances. For example, a best practice for GE

73

or Toyota or Cisco may not be best for a smaller company with fewer resources or a totally different approach to research or production. As I have done research into training methods in different companies, I have collected what I call excellent practices. These are well-documented, effective practices that may offer ideas and alternative approaches that should be considered by other companies, given their needs, circumstances, and constraints, but not automatically accepted as the best for them.

Critical thinking is designed not to limit possibilities but to open new possibilities that are unconstrained by rigid beliefs and false assumptions. In this way, critical thinking can open you to creative thinking.

Creative Thinking

Creativity is the process of bringing into existence something that did not exist before, either a product, a process, or an idea. The result of creative thinking may be to

- Invent something that has never existed before (at least to your knowledge—if you don't know something exists, it doesn't exist for you)
- Invent a new way of doing something
- Apply an existing product, process, or idea to a different market or use it in a different way
- Change the way that you, or others, look at a problem or challenge

You need to focus on overcoming those things that restrain you from thinking creatively:

- Your beliefs and assumptions may restrain you from examining new ideas, so you can use critical thinking to examine those restraints.
- You may have been taught in school that there is only one correct way to solve a problem, so you are hesitant to try something new.
- You may be unwilling to try something new if old methods are working for you.

You need to remember that progress is never made by doing the same things the same ways you have always done them. Of course, you need to judge how much risk you are willing to take and what levels of risk are acceptable to your manager and your company.

....

I once worked in a marketing group whose manager had come from outside the company. He encouraged everyone in the group to try new things, and if someone tried something new and it worked well, he showered that person with praise and rewards in the form of bonuses, salary increases, stock options, and promotions. If a person tried something new and didn't succeed, the manager didn't fire her, but he made it clear that the person should look for a new job, either elsewhere in the company or on the outside.

As a result, the only people who really took the risk of trying something new were those who were confident, both that their creative approach would work and that, if it didn't, they wouldn't have a problem in finding a new job. For those people, their work was a wonderful adventure; for those who were risk-averse, their creative ideas never saw the light of day because they never wanted to risk having to find a new job.

....

Stifling Creativity

How do individuals stifle their own creativity and that of others? There are many ways that this is done every day. Think about the last time you participated in a group problem-solving session. You may have come to the meeting with your own solution in mind. Your goal for the meeting was to get your solution accepted by the others. Why did you start with this strategy? It may have been because

* You wanted others to recognize your brilliance.
* The solution you were offering was within your comfort zone, that is, you could accomplish it with the capabilities you had at that moment, so the solution was very safe for you.

If you are not the first to be asked for a solution, you don't really listen to other ideas but merely wait your turn to present your own. While others take their turns to give their solutions to the problem, you ignore them or, worse, you try to subvert them so that yours will rise to the top, almost by default. For each of the other offered solutions, you dismiss them by using idea killers, such as

- "That will never work here."
- "I tried that before, and it didn't work."
- "Where did that crazy notion come from?"

When you finally get your turn to offer your idea, you are surprised that other people don't immediately accept it as perfect. You have your ego invested in your solution, and you want to avoid the risk, inherent in other ideas, that someone else will be regarded as smarter than you. If everyone in the group starts with this same attitude, the meeting will almost never come up with the optimal solution that might be reached by combining the ideas offered by several people in the group.

Nurture Your Own Creativity

Daniel Pink predicts that the future will belong to the creative, and that right-brained individuals will be more valued than left-brain thinkers.[3] The left side of the human brain is associated with logic, while the right side is associated with creativity. Every person uses both sides of the brain, but in some people the left side dominates, while in others the right side is dominant. As Pink explains, you can develop your right brain, or creative side, by actively nurturing your creative abilities. Here are some ways that you can build them.

Get to Know and Understand Your Strengths and Weaknesses.

Every individual has strong and weak points. Increase your self-knowledge by getting to know and understand where yours lie. It is understandable to seek solutions to problems that focus on your own strengths, but just because you are comfortable with a solution doesn't automatically mean that it is the best possible one. If you identify your weaknesses, you can try to develop yourself in those areas, although some would argue that you cannot always overcome inherent weaknesses.

Chuck Martin and his coauthors argue that our brains are hardwired and that there are some abilities that we may never be able to develop fully because our "wiring" is wrong.[4] For example, if you are a disorganized person and have an office that is full of stacks of books and paper (as mine is), it may be that your brain just isn't wired to support neatness. Although you may read books and take workshops on organization, it is likely that you will never become a truly organized person. One solution to such a situation is to partner with someone who is wired for those skills and who can help you with your organization. For example, at one company, a brilliant marketing executive was highly valued for her ideas. But because of hardwired learning disabilities, she was a very poor speller, and the company feared what customers would think if they ever received a letter or e-mail from her that was full of atrocious errors. Because the company regarded her marketing ideas so highly, the management hired an assistant for her who had been an English major, and every letter, report, and e-mail was screened and edited by the assistant before being sent out.

Similarly, if you find that there is some aspect of creative thinking in which you are not adept, one solution would be to partner with someone in your company who has strength in that area. In fact, I believe that an often-overlooked aspect of diversity is differences in thinking styles. Whenever I hire people or put together a team, I always try to incorporate a wide spectrum of thinking styles so people can build on one another's ideas from a variety of vantage points. By aligning yourself with people whose strengths are different from your own, you can build on your strengths and compensate for your weaknesses.

Keep Current in Your Field.

The rate of knowledge creation in today's world has increased, and will continue to increase exponentially. Since you attended school to learn the skills you use in your work, the knowledge in your field of endeavor has multiplied every year. Even if you are only a few years out of school, there has been a whole new body of knowledge created since your graduation. With the electronic resources available on the World Wide Web today, access to that knowledge is easier than ever.

Here are a few ways you can keep up to date:

- Read magazines, journals, and other literature in your field to ensure that you are not using yesterday's solutions to solve today's problems.
- Join the professional society for your profession—most fields have them. Attend local chapter meetings and, if you can, national conferences. Spend time at trade shows to see what others in your field are doing. Become active on discussion boards relating to your work.

79

- Share your knowledge and skills with other members of your group, and ask them to share theirs with you. A newly hired college graduate may have 5 or 10 or 20 years less experience than you do, but she is probably more current on the state of the art in your profession because she has been exposed to it more recently. Meet regularly with others who do your same job within the company. Each member of your group has different education and different experiences from yours, so take the time to learn from one another and you will all benefit. Look beyond your education for new ideas. If Albert Einstein had relied totally on what he learned during his years in school, he would never have devised the theory of relativity. As he once said, "The only thing that interferes with my learning is my education."

Expand Your Horizons Beyond Your Own Specialty.

No one works in isolation. You have suppliers and customers for your work. Your suppliers are those who give you the information or material you use in doing your work. Your customers are those people to whom you give your completed work so that they can do theirs. For most people, your suppliers and customers will be inside your organization rather than external to it.

Take the time to learn about the value chain and the major business processes within your own company. Spend some time learning about the specialties of other employees who are involved in the overall process—learning about how another specialist handles his or her own work may spark ideas on how to improve your own.

Watch and Listen.

Listen to others' ideas, and watch how they do their work. In meetings, ask yourself if you are really listening or just waiting for your turn to talk. As former U.S. President Lyndon B. Johnson once said, "You aren't learning anything when you are talking." And to quote Yogi Berra, "You can observe a lot by just watching."

Don't dismiss other people's ideas or ways of accomplishing their work just because they are different from yours. When you hear an idea or see a different way of working, try to overcome any biases or preconceived notions, and look for ways in which you could benefit from using all or part of what you are observing. If another person's idea or work method is not fully developed, help her develop it further by exploring similarities, differences, and possibilities for using all or part of it in your own work.

Keep Track of Your Own Ideas.

Ideas may come to you at any time: at work, at home, or waking in the night. Keep a record of all the ideas that occur to you—if you don't write them down, you are going to lose them. In this book's appendix, you will learn about keeping a personal learning journal, which is an ideal place to keep track of your ideas.

Once you have an idea, pursue it. Try it out in your work or by discussing it with your manager or others in your group. Be open to suggestions from others, and get others to help you develop your ideas. They will be especially open to helping you develop your ideas if you are mutually supportive of their ideas.

Even though an idea itself may ultimately prove impractical, there may be parts or facets of it that can be combined with other ideas to yield excellent results. But you will never make progress if you dismiss your own ideas and those from others without investing time in their discussion and development.

Practice, Practice, Practice.

Creativity is a learned skill set. You can augment your creative skills by spending time on creative hobbies. While a hobby may not be directly related to your job, a creative hobby can help develop your right brain's creative muscle.

Another vital facet of creativity is the habit of asking questions. Start each workday by asking yourself a new question: What if I were to ... ? How can I get this task done faster? Do I need to expend so much money on this project, or is there a more economical solution? Nobel laureate Jacob Bronowski states that this is the essence of science: "Ask an impertinent question and you are on the way to a pertinent answer."

Use questioning to explore possibilities, not just for your own ideas, but for ideas you get from others. Make certain that the purpose and tone of your questions are aimed at better understanding and finding new possibilities, rather than sniping at others' ideas

> *A prudent question is one-half of wisdom.*
> —Francis Bacon

just because they are not your own. When others ask questions about your thoughts, don't view it as a personal attack, but as an attempt to better understand your idea and to help your develop it further. Keep yourself open to new possibilities.

Be a Risk Taker.

Nothing in life is certain (except death and taxes, as the old adage goes). You need to trust your creativity enough to take measured risks. This does not mean that you

> *One of the reasons people stop learning is that they become less and less willing to risk failure.*
>
> —John W. Gardner

should become foolhardy, but that you should test and stretch your own risk-taking limits. If you never try anything new, you will never progress beyond where you are now.

You also need to judge the risk-tolerance levels of your manager and your organization. As John Kotter states: "Bureaucratic and risk-averse environments are career killers because of their impact on learning." You can lower your risk by talking with your manager before starting on a new path, explaining what you want to try, and asking for some leeway in the manager's evaluation of your work in case your idea doesn't pan out.

Creative experimentation will always end up with some measure of failure. Things don't always work out the way we have envisioned. You cannot be a risk taker and a perfectionist at the same time. The risk taker is open to learning; the perfectionist is not. As stated by E. J. Phelps, "The man who makes no mistakes does not usually make anything."

Keep Your Sense of Humor.

Finally, keep your sense of humor. Levity can open the pathways to creativity and help you keep your problems in perspective. Humor, appropriately applied, can relieve tension, make you more relaxed, and open your mind to new ideas.

Chapter Summary

In this chapter, we have explored critical and creative thinking, and provided you with some guidance on how to develop and utilize your critical and creative thinking skills. Being a perfectionist closes you off from new ideas and from examining how to improve your own, your group's, and your organization's performance. The reason why some people are perfectionists is that they are very risk-averse. That is, they feel safer doing things in the same ways they have always done them and fear that if they try something new, they will fail.

While an individual can be creative when working alone, it can be very helpful to share your creative ideas with others, asking for their help in developing your ideas and, at the same time, helping them develop theirs. Often, the best solution to a problem can come from considering a combination of ideas.

If you want to develop your critical and creative thinking skills further, you can find a number of references in the book's bibliography that can help you.

In the next chapter, we will look further at the role of experimentation as a learning method: learning from trial and error.

Notes

1. Stephen D. Brookfield, *Developing Critical Thinkers* (Jossey-Bass, 1983).
2. Ibid. pp. 22–23.
3. Daniel Pink, *A Whole New Mind* (Riverhead Trade, 2006).
4. Chuck Martin, *Smarts: Are We Hardwired for Success?* (AMACOM, 2007).

CHAPTER

5

EXPERIMENTING:
LEARN FROM TRIAL AND ERROR

There are three principal means
of acquiring knowledge . . .
observation of nature, reflection,
and experimentation. Observation
collects facts; reflection combines
them; experimentation verifies
the result of that combination.

—Denis Diderot

Think back to the model of the Four Stages of Learning (see Figure 1-1). Stage 4 of learning is wisdom. Wisdom is developed through dialogue, demonstration, experience, intuition, and experimentation. As you gain experience in using your knowledge and skills, you may think of new ways of applying your learning and experience and experiment to see what happens if you change one or more parameters. Also, remember that before you get to wisdom, you have to pass through Stage

3, knowledge. You develop knowledge from applying what you learn to your work. Only after you have mastered your work should you start experimenting.

Experimenting is essentially trying something different. In conducting an experiment, it is important to start with a hypothesis. A hypothesis is a theory that by combining certain facts, you can explain a result. You test a hypothesis by using an experiment. As a simple example, you can experiment with a recipe, testing a new combination of flavors or ingredients to see if you like the result: "I like chocolate, and I like anchovies. My hypothesis is that if I combine these two foods, I will come up with a new recipe that I like." Your experiment is then to combine the two ingredients in a new dish, taste the result, and see if you like it.

It is important to plan your experiment and keep a record of it. If you enjoyed the hot-fudge pizza with anchovies, you will want to keep a record of the recipe so that you can replicate it in the future. If you didn't like the result, you will want to keep a record so that you don't suffer through trying the same thing in the future. Whether your experiment succeeds or fails, you will have learned something from the experience; you should share your learning with others so that they can either try the recipe or avoid combining chocolate and anchovies in a pizza themselves.

When you conduct an experiment, sometimes the results are positive. More often, they are negative. And sometimes an experiment leads to a totally unexpected but useful result. Whether the experiment succeeds or fails, it creates new information, and if you use that information in your work, it becomes your personal knowledge. In inventing the incandescent lightbulb, Thomas Edison tried 10,000 different elements before finding that tungsten would work for the filament. He did not consider the 10,000 trials as failures, but as the discovery of 10,000 things that didn't work and the one that did.

The Invention of Post-it Notes

One of the best-selling office products today is Post-it Notes, made by 3M. They were not a planned product. In 1970, a 3M scientist, Spencer Silver, was working on developing a strong adhesive, but he found that what he had created was even weaker than the company's existing products. The experiment failed: the adhesive stuck to objects, but it could easily be lifted off. Silver filed away the new discovery in his lab notes and went on with other experiments to create a stronger adhesive.

Four years later, another 3M scientist, Arthur Fry, was singing in his church's choir. He had put slips of paper in his hymnal to mark the location of particular hymns, but the slips kept falling out. Fry remembered the weak adhesive that Spencer Silver had developed, and that became the solution to his problem: when he put the weak adhesive on slips of paper, they would stay in place; however, he could later remove them without damaging the pages.

Even with this new use of Silver's discovery, 3M was not convinced that there was a market for such a product. After prototypes were made and distributed to 3M employees, they proved wildly popular, and since their introduction in the early 1980s, they have evolved into a product line of more than 4,000 products.

An insurance company was concerned that its customer satisfaction ratings for claims adjusters were very low. The company had experimented with many different types of training for the adjusters, mainly focused on how to assess the value of a client's loss. Most of it resulted in little, if any, change in the customers' ratings. The solution the company finally found was to educate the adjusters on empathy skills. Once the empathy training was completed, customers' satisfaction ratings of the adjusters immediately jumped significantly. Clients who had experienced an insured loss, whether for a loved one's life, an automobile accident, or storm damage to their homes, were already upset enough before dealing with their insurance company to make a claim. They wanted some sympathy, not just an estimate of their reimbursement.

The whole quality movement has "continuous improvement" at its heart. Continuous improvement is simply a continuing series of experiments to make minor adjustments to improve quality. In the Toyota Manufacturing System, the best-known benchmark for a manufacturing quality program, any worker on the factory floor can stop the manufacturing process at any time to try a new idea to improve quality. Most of these experiments fail, but many succeed; even the ones that fail result in learning.

> *The biggest job we have is to teach a newly hired employee how to fail intelligently. We have to train him to experiment over and over and to keep on trying and failing until he learns what will work.*
> —Charles F. Kettering

Design of Experiments

We often think of experimentation as being in the realm of science. Scientific research, based on theory, performs many experiments to test the validity of its premises. There is a whole field of study called "design of experiments" that details strict methodologies to test hypotheses. If you are working in a scientific field, your professional standards require you to follow these methodologies.

What we want to focus on here are not the large scientific experiments that result in a new technology or a new drug, but the improvement of your work methods in your current job in small ways—ways that you can try yourself. Here are the six steps you should follow in conducting these types of experiments.

1.   Form a hypothesis. What idea do you have for improving your job performance? Write it down. For instance, "I think that if I alter this procedure in the following way, I can save time or reduce costs or improve quality." Don't try to make too many changes at once. If you do, you may not be able to tell which of those modifications is having a real effect on your performance. If you have many ideas for changes, form multiple hypotheses that you can test singly or in small, related groups.

2.   Discuss your hypothesis with your group and your manager. Get their ideas and listen to their reactions to your hypothesis—open yourself to learning from their knowledge and experience. They may be able to help you sharpen your hypothesis, or they may tell you that they have already tried what you are proposing.

3. Design an experiment. How will you test your hypothesis? What are you going to change? How will you measure your results? Will you need help from others to conduct the experiment? What will happen if the experiment fails? (You want to avoid potentially disastrous results.) For how long will you conduct the experiment? Will you have a control group to help you measure the changes resulting from the experiment?

4. Review your design with your manager and other group members. They may have ideas on how to improve your design, or they may see a potentially fatal flaw in your design. In any case, you will want to get approval from your manager for the experiment.

5. Conduct the experiment, and record your results. At the end of your experiment, you should have a complete record of what you did and what the results were. Whether they are positive or negative, write down what you learned.

6. Share your findings with your manager and your group. Share what you learned. If your results were positive, make a recommendation for a permanent change in the group's work methods. If your results were negative, tell them what you learned. This will help them avoid trying the same thing themselves. If your results were inconclusive, you may want to work with your manager and your group to try something else. If Spencer Silver had not reported the negative results of his experiment, Post-it Notes would never have been invented. As Thomas Edison said, "Just because something doesn't do what you planned it to do doesn't mean it's useless."

Barriers to Experimentation

What keeps us from experimenting? Fear of failure or risk aversion can affect your ability and willingness to experiment. These characteristics can be found at the organizational level, at the work group level (your manager), or at a personal level.

Risk-Averse Organizations

Is your company very bureaucratic, with many layers of approvals required for even the most minor change? If so, then the company has established an environment in which experimentation will be extremely limited. Either the process of getting approval to experiment is so burdensome that few people actually ask for permission or the penalties established for going outside standard operating procedures are so extreme that few people are willing to take the risk of doing so and being found out.

....

My first job at a high-tech company was in its educational services division. This division had been developing and delivering training the same way for more than 20 years, and it had a five-inch binder that codified all its methods, from how to conduct a needs assessment to the typefaces to be used in student materials. Over my first few years in the company, it became clear to me that this methodology was not working well for the product group that I supported. After doing my own needs analysis of the training needed by the sales and support staff for this product set, I developed an alternative approach to providing the needed training, an experimental approach that was unique not just for the

91

company but also for the industry. When I brought my new ideas to the educational services management team, they told me that their methodology was not open to discussion or modification.

Because I couldn't do what I felt was needed within the educational services group, I went to work for the product-marketing group to test the new methodology. While the first program I developed using the new methodology was well received by the audience, some aspects were more successful than others, and it still needed more work. I tried a number of modifications over the next few sessions, learning through trial and error what worked well and what didn't. At the same time, even though these new programs were becoming more and more successful, the management of the educational services group refused to reexamine their methodology and aggressively lobbied the company's senior leadership to stop my efforts because they didn't conform to their way of doing things.

The educational services group was not a division that was open to experimentation. Even though the ratings and the results from the new model were very high, the educational services management team refused to consider any changes to their model. Over time, other marketing groups within the company replicated the new model, but they had to conduct the programs themselves, rather than under the umbrella of educational services.

Compare this type of organization with a company like 3M, which allows employees to spend a portion of every workweek experimenting on personal projects. In such an organization, experimentation is not just encouraged but expected. 3M and similar companies know that innovation is their lifeblood, and that the more people experiment and learn through their experimentation, the more profitable the company will become.

Of course, there are organizations and work groups that must be very risk-averse and, as a result, limit experimentation. If you work for a nuclear power plant, you shouldn't be planning any experiment that might result in a core meltdown, no matter how small the probability of that outcome. Similarly, if you work for an aircraft manufacturer, any experiment you plan should not have the remotest possibility of causing an airplane crash. That is why these types of industries spend large amounts of money to create simulators where it doesn't matter if an experiment fails, because it all happens in an artificial environment rather than in real life.

If you work for a company that prohibits experimentation or makes it extremely difficult to do, you won't be learning as much as you can, and this will eventually limit your job and career possibilities. Of course, if you yourself are very risk-averse and want a job where you can just keep doing the same things in the same ways forever, this type of company may be right for you.

> Bureaucratic and risk-averse environments are career killers because of their impact on learning.
>
> —John Kotter

93

Risk-Averse Managers

Even if your company encourages experimentation, you may have a manager who is risk-averse. Your manager may be a know-it-all who won't abide any questioning or discussion of the work procedures he has put in place. Or he may worry that if the experiments don't succeed, he will not be able to meet his group's work quotas. If you work for such a person, you should realize that you probably won't learn much while working for him and that this may limit your job and career aspirations.

Are You Risk-Averse?

Do you fear making a mistake or having a negative outcome from an experiment? Perfectionists rarely experiment. They have found ways of getting their work done within the boundaries set by their manager, and they are very happy to continue using the same work methods that allow them to continue to do their work properly. They don't want to mess with what is working for them for fear of making an error. Albert Einstein said, "A person who never made a mistake never tried anything new." While you may welcome the safety of the status quo, if you are not experimenting and are not open to new ideas, you are limiting your ability to learn and your potential for growing in your job and your career.

Ways to Overcome Your Fear of Failure

If you find yourself unwilling to experiment because you fear that you will fail, here are some ways to help you overcome that trepidation.

> It is hard to fail, but it is worse never to have tried to succeed.
> —Theodore Roosevelt

- Consider the cost of missed opportunities. Netscape founder Marc Andreessen wrote: "The issue is that without taking risk, you can't exploit any opportunities. You can live a quiet and reasonably happy life, but you are unlikely to create something new, and you are unlikely to make your mark on the world."

- Before experimenting, do your homework. Take the time to define the problem you are trying to solve. Is it a one-time occurrence, or is there a pattern that you can identify? Once you have identified the problem, take time to consider all your alternatives and research the potential outcomes, both positive and negative, for each alternative. Discuss the problem and the alternatives with your manager and your coworkers. Perhaps one of them has already faced the same problem and come up with a workable solution. Research any articles in magazines or journals that may discuss your specific problem or similar issues to see what alternatives others have tried and the results.

- Plan your experiment. What will you do? How will you do it? When will you do it? What results are you seeking? How will you measure those results? What will success look like?

- Persist! Don't give up. If one alternative doesn't work, try another. Successful people keep trying. Thomas Edison said, "Our greatest weakness lies in giving up. The most certain way to succeed is always to try just one more time."

- Don't be too hard on yourself. If nothing else, your experiment will teach you what doesn't work. Remember that having a failed experiment does not mean that you are a failure—no one succeeds all the time or even most of the time. The best baseball players may have a batting average of .400, but that means that they succeed in getting a hit only two in every five chances. Hockey great Wayne Gretzky's career shooting percentage was 17.57 percent, meaning that he missed 82.43 percent of the shots he took. Gretzky states: "You miss 100 percent of the shots you don't take."

- Remember that all experiments are opportunities to learn. If your experiment fails, ask yourself:

  o What went wrong?
  o Why did it happen?
  o How could the negative result have been prevented?
  o How can I do better next time?

No one can be right all the time—not you, not your manager, not your CEO. Progress in any field requires experimentation, and experimentation will usually lead to more wrong answers than right ones. In order to learn,

> *Our doubts are traitors, and make us lose the good we oft might win by fearing to attempt.*
> —William Shakespeare

you need to open yourself to new ideas, methods, and ways of thinking. Only then will you make progress.

Chapter Summary

Experimenting, using trial and error, is a major way in which people learn. To learn from experimentation, you need to formulate hypotheses and then develop experiments to test them. Whether your experiment is successful or unsuccessful, you should learn from the experience. Risk aversion, or fear of failure, is a major barrier to experimentation—some organizations have risk-averse environments, or sometimes it may be the manager who is risk-averse. If you find yourself in a company or working for a manager that does not allow experimentation, you should realize that these conditions will impede your learning and may hold back your job and career progression. If you find yourself paralyzed by the fear of failure, proper preparation for experimenting and realization that even negative results lead to learning can help you overcome that fear.

ASKING QUESTIONS:
BE A SMART DUMMY

> *Asking a question is the simplest
> way of focusing thinking . . .
> asking the right question may
> be the most important part of
> thinking.*
>
> —Edward de Bono

*A senior executive at a consumer product goods company
told me that whenever he puts together a problem-solving
team, he always makes certain that the team includes a
smart dummy. When I asked him to define "smart dummy," he said that it is a very bright person who has no background or knowledge about the problem, someone who can
ask naive questions.*

*The example the executive gave me was of a team he
had appointed to find ways to reduce the shipping costs that*

ran the company tens of millions of dollars per year. Most of the members of the team were from the logistics department. The smart dummy, who was from an unrelated department, asked the team: "How do we know that we are getting the lowest shipping rates from our vendors?" The vice president of logistics replied, "Because our rates are below the vendors' published rates." The smart dummy then asked if they had ever requested additional discounts from the freight companies.

Because of this naive question, the vice president of logistics called the vendors to ask if the rates could be lowered and was immediately given additional discounts that saved the company several million dollars a year. If the smart dummy had not asked this question, the new discounts would never have been requested or offered.

There is no such thing as a dumb question. If you are puzzled by something, or if you are not certain you understand what has been said or what you have seen or read, you aren't going to learn anything if you don't ask for an explanation.

Most people are reluctant to ask questions because they feel that they should already know the answer and don't want to appear ignorant or naive. You were hired to do a particular job. You probably

> *I have learned the novice can often see things that the expert overlooks. All that is necessary is not to be afraid of making mistakes, or of appearing naive.*
> —Abraham Maslow

told the hiring manager that you are perfectly capable of doing that job. Now, if you start asking naive questions, you may fear that the hiring manager will either think that you lied about your qualifications or question whether she made the right decision in giving you the position. It can be a blow to your ego to admit that you don't know something, or know how to do something, that your manager believes you should know.

What you need to realize is that asking questions, even if they seem naive to you, is the major way that you will learn at work. No one knows everything, and with the exponential growth of information, even if you know everything you need to know right now, it will soon be out of date. Even if you think it is something you should know, you can fake it for only so long before you are discovered—better to ask your question the first time it arises than to let people think you know something that you don't or can do something that you can't.

> *He who asks a question may be a fool for five minutes. But he who never asks a question remains a fool forever.*
> —Tom J. Connelly

Learning Your Company's Jargon

When you start work in an organization that's new to you, you need to learn its jargon. The jargon may consist of shortcut names for company products or processes that are commonly used, or phrases that are particular to that company's culture. For example, when I first started working for a major computer company, I often heard people say in meetings, "Let's not go down that rat-hole," and "Let's handle that offline." What the "rat-hole" phrase meant was that someone's comment or issue was off-topic and, if pursued in the meeting, would take the discussion in an unknown direction. Handling something "offline" meant that they should talk about the topic in a personal discussion outside the meeting. Nevertheless, I would not have understood these phrases if I hadn't asked someone what they meant.

There will also be acronyms that are commonly used as shortcuts. Every business has them, and government agencies seem to have more than their share—you won't know what they mean unless you inquire. You may not want to interrupt a meeting to find the meaning of the local patois or an acronym, but you should write your questions down and later ask your manager or a coworker—you'll soon be fluent in the language of the organization.

Types of Questions

There are four basic types of questions you can ask:

1. Closed questions
2. Open-ended questions
3. Fact-finding questions
4. Follow-up questions

Let's look at each type.

Closed Questions

Closed questions are specific and must be answered with a yes or no, or with details if necessary. "Is the report ready?" "Did you solve that customer's complaint?" "When will you have that drawing ready?" Closed questions seek a particular answer and result in the fastest response. They also do not open the topic for any discussion.

Open-Ended Questions

Open-ended questions do not require a particular response, such as yes or no, but open the topic for discussion. Instead of asking, "Is the report ready?" a related open-ended question would be, "How is the report coming along?" or, "Why is your project behind schedule?" Open-ended questions invite different opinions, the discussion of the issues involved, and creative problem solving. They often start with *how, why,* or "What do you think about … " They take more time to handle than closed questions because you are not seeking just a yes or no answer but are asking for more information and opinions.

Fact-Finding Questions

Fact-finding questions are intended to gather more information on a particular subject. A new hire may ask her manager or a colleague, "How do I fill out my time sheet?" For example, in a previous story, I told how I was preparing a report and had a bunch of data in a spreadsheet program that I wanted to make into charts and graphs, but I didn't know how to do it. I went to a colleague who was an expert on creating the types of charts and graphs I wanted and asked him to show me how to generate what I needed—this was a fact-finding question. I could have spent hours with the spreadsheet program's help screens or poring through the thick user's manual, but asking the expert how to do it resulted in a 30-minute tutorial that taught me what I needed to get the job done.

Follow-Up Questions

These types of queries are designed to elicit more information than the questioner received in a previous answer. If you have watched a presidential news conference, a reporter will often ask a question, listen to the president's response, and then ask a follow-up question to get a more detailed answer or more information on one aspect of the answer. Similarly, an employee may ask a manager for help in solving a problem. The manager may issue a quick response, starting with, "Here's what you should do." A follow-up question might be, "Can you explain why that is the right answer, so I can learn from this?"

Asking Questions and Getting Answers from the Employee's View

Asking questions to gather knowledge is a major learning method for employees at all levels of an organization. In Chapter 3, a scenario was discussed where an employee asked his or her manager for help in solving a problem or in understanding something. The scenario presented five potential responses from the manager:

1. "Don't bother me. Figure it out yourself."
2. "Just leave it with me, and I'll take care of it."
3. "Here's what you need to do."
4. "Let me show you how to do that."
5. "What do you think you ought to do?"

As discussed in Chapter 3, the first two answers do not present opportunities to learn, and the employee should use follow-up questions to learn more. Answer #3 gets the problem solved, but doesn't lead to a greater understanding of why the manager's solution is the correct one and how the employee could reach the same conclusion in the future. This type of response should result in follow-up questions from the employee. "Let me show you how to do that" provides greater learning.

The fifth answer, "What do you think you ought to do?" can lead to the greatest learning for both the employee and the manager—it is an empowering question. As Judith Ross, writing in the *Harvard Business Review* blog, states: "[A]n empowering question does more than convey respect for the person to which it's posed. It actually encourages that person's development as a thinker and problem solver, thereby delivering both short-term and long-term value: the short-term value of generating a solution to the issue at hand and the long-term value of giving subordinates the tools to handle similar issues in the future."[1]

The tone of a question (and an answer) also carries a lot of weight with any employee. "How did you reach that conclusion?" will lead to more learning than "Why did you do a dumb thing like that?" The first and second manager responses above generally show impatience and imply an unwillingness to help the employee learn, and they may discourage the employee from asking questions in the future.

Asking Yourself Questions

Marilee Adams of the Inquiry Institute has spent many years studying the field of questioning. She has compiled a list of the

"Top 12 Questions" (see Figure 6-1). These types of questions can help any employee determine how to overcome the challenges he faces in his work. Not every question is applicable to every situation, but when you find yourself stuck, start by going through the list and see which questions can help you make progress. Another approach is called "optimal thinking," which says that in any difficult situation where you may have many options open to you, you should ask yourself, "What's the best thing I can do right now to resolve this issue?"[2]

---

1. What do I want?
2. What are my choices?
3. What assumptions am I making?
4. What am I responsible for?
5. How else can I think about this?
6. What is the other person thinking, feeling, needing and wanting?
7. What am I missing or avoiding?
8. What can I learn
   - from this person or situation?
   - from this mistake or failure?
   - from this success?
9. What action steps make the most sense?
10. What questions should I ask (myself or others)?
11. How can I turn this into a win-win situation?
12. What is possible?

Source: The Inquiry Institute, http://inquiryinstitute.com/resources/top-12-questions/.

FIGURE 6-1: Top 12 Questions from The Inquiry Institute

The Manager's View of Asking and Answering Questions

When an employee asks a manager a question, the manager is concerned with how much time it will take to answer the question to get the issue resolved and how much the employee will learn from the answer. Using the same five responses listed above, Table 6-1 reflects the manager's time commitment and the potential for learning for each response.

Manager's Response to Employee's Question	Manager's Time Commitment	Potential for Employee Learning
"Don't bother me. Figure it out yourself!"	★	None
"Just leave it with me, and I'll take care of it."	★	None
"Here's what you need to do."	★★	★
"Let me show you how to do that."	★★★	★★★
"What do you think you ought to do?"	★★★★★	★★★★★

TABLE 6-1: Manager's Time Commitment vs. Potential for Employee Learning

The first response ("Don't bother me. Figure it out yourself.") requires very little of the manager's time. The second response ("Just leave it with me, and I'll take care of it.") implies that it will take less time for the manager to take care of it himself than to explain how to solve the problem to the employee. Both of these responses result in no employee learning and her being dependent on the manager each time she faces a similar situation. The third response, "Here's what you need to do," takes more time than the first two and may enable the employee to learn what to do if the same situation arises again. There are times when any of these may be the right answer to a question—for example, if there is an immediate safety issue and a quick response is needed, or if it is a unique situation that is unlikely to arise again.

The fourth response, "Let me show you how to do that," teaches the employee how to solve the problem. The manager's explanation can be brief ("Do these steps ... "), or it can require more time if the manager instructs the employee on how to think about the problem, what alternatives to consider, and how to select the best choice. This response takes more of the manager's time than any of the first three responses, but it will result in more learning and a greater probability that the next time the employee faces a similar situation, he will be able to diagnose and solve the problem without taking more of the manager's time.

The fifth response ("What do you think you ought to do?") answers a question with a question and implies a coaching approach. It is designed to empower the employee, as Judith Ross stated in her *Harvard Business Review* blog. She suggests that managers who use empowering questions "create value in one of more of the following ways:

1. They create clarity: "Can you explain more about this situation?"
2. They construct better working relations: instead of "Did you make your sales goal?" ask, "How have sales been going?"
3. They help people think analytically and critically: "What are the consequences of going this route?"
4. They inspire people to reflect and see things in fresh, unpredictable ways: "Why did this work?"
5. They encourage breakthrough thinking: "Can that be done in any other way?"
6. They challenge assumptions: "What do you think you will lose if you start sharing responsibility for the implementation process?"
7. They create ownership of solutions: "Based on your experience, what do you suggest we do here?"[3]

The point of coaching is to help the employee develop thinking, problem analysis, and decision-making skills. It does not imply that the manager doesn't know what to do, although the coaching questions can help both the employee and the manager analyze a problem if neither has a ready solution. Asking coaching questions should never be used to force an employee to select the solution that the manager already has in mind. A manager should never keep asking the employee to suggest a solution and keep the employee guessing at alternative solutions until the employee comes up with the one the manager wants—that's not coaching, it's manipulation. Of course, there are times when a manager needs to impose a solution, for example, when there is a safety risk or a regulatory issue that requires a specific solution. In these cases, the manager should select option 3

("Here's what you need to do") and explain to the employee the reasons why this is the only acceptable solution.

Exploratory Questions

Sometimes you ask questions not to get a specific answer, but to explore possibilities. These types of questions need to be asked with the right tone and in the right spirit. Otherwise, the person you are questioning may see these questions as hostile. In addition, while you may really like the idea you have created, it doesn't mean that everyone else's ideas should immediately be dismissed—you don't always need to be the smartest person in the room! So when you are exchanging ideas, use exploratory questions to learn more. Consider the phrases in Table 6.2, which are often used to stifle ideas and alternative questions that can be used to explore those ideas.

Stifling Comment	Exploratory Question
That will never work here!	How would that work here?
What were you thinking?	Tell me how you arrived at that solution?
We tried that before and it didn't work.	When we tried that before, what kept it from working?
We haven't got the (time, budget, manpower) to do that.	How can we do this given the constraints on (time, budget, manpower)?
Yes, but . . .	Yes, and . . .

Table 6-2: From Stifling Comment to Exploratory Questions

In Chapter 4, we discussed critical and creative thinking. With regard to critical thinking, we want to uncover any biases, assumptions, and constraints that affect our solution to a problem. Exploratory questions can do just that. For example:

- When given a new assignment, you can ask your manager what constraints are in place that you should keep in mind in developing a solution.
- You can ask someone how she came up with her solution to a problem, what other solutions she considered, and why the alternative solutions were not selected.

Exploratory questions are most effective when they are used to spark creative thinking. Don't get fixated on your own idea or solution—explore alternatives using the types of exploratory questions listed in Figure 6-1 (see page 106)—not only will you learn more, but your colleagues will appreciate your helping them think through their ideas and improve on them.

....

A new group manager was hired from outside the company. In his first few staff meetings, he peppered his direct reports with questions about the projects they were working on. The staff got very uncomfortable. Finally, one staff member asked to speak with the new manager in private. "I need to tell you that you are making your staff very uncomfortable. Your constant questions about our projects imply that you don't trust us and that you are going to be a micromanager."

The manager thanked him for letting him know about the distressing questions. "I guess I should have told people that all my questions are not aimed at finding fault but to improve my understanding of what the group is doing. I'm new here, and I need to learn about all our current projects. My questions are to help me learn, not to intimidate or second-guess anyone on the staff."

Yes, there are some micromanagers in the world who question every detail of their staff's work. However, more often, the manager's questions are designed to improve understanding and to help people think through their plans and actions to help them learn as well.

Chapter Summary

Asking questions is a major learning method that you can use on the job every single day. You shouldn't hesitate to ask questions for fear that you will expose your ignorance, but should eagerly ask questions to learn. Questioning is a vital component of both critical and creative thinking. Exploratory questions can not only help the questioner better understand another person's ideas, but also help that person to consider alternatives and improve those ideas. You should never be intimidated from asking questions, nor should you be unsettled by questions asked of you—both are meant to help you learn.

Notes

1. Judith Ross, http://blogs.hbr.org/hmu/2009/05/real-leaders-ask.html.
2. See Rosalene Glickman, *Optimal Thinking* (Wiley, 2002).
3. Judith Ross, op. cit.

DEFINING TEAMS BY WHAT THEY LEARN

C ommon definitions of a team include these elements:

- A group of people who have a common goal
- A group of people whose work is interdependent
- A group of people who have joint responsibility and accountability for results

I add to this list:

- Team members either learn from one another or learn together to accomplish their goals

The point here is that unless there is learning taking place among team members, or unless the team members are together learning something new, there really isn't a team but just a group of people who happen to work for the same manager.

....

Bob and Fred were trainers at a Fortune 500 company and specialized in team training. A manager had asked them to give their workshop to the eight members of her team. On the first day of the three-day program, the employees assembled in the training room. Fred asked them to describe their team goals. Silence. "How long have you been working as a team?" asked Fred. Silence. "What's the biggest challenge you have in working as a team?" Silence.

Finally, one of the employees spoke up: "We're not a team. We each have our own work to do: individual assignments given by our manager. We're expected to do our own work and get called on the carpet if she sees two or more of us talking with each other."

The two trainers did what I believe was the right thing, and something that most in their job would not do: they dismissed the class and went to talk with the manager, explaining what it meant to have a team rather than a group of people who happen to work for the same person. If she wanted to have her group work as a team, they told her, she would first have to learn how to be a team leader.

....

Bob and Fred knew that using any or all of the definitions of team, this was not a team but a work group. The major differences between a team and work group are given in Table 7-1.

Let's look at some examples of teams to illustrate how they differ from work groups.

In a Team	In a Work Group
Leadership is shared among team members	There is one manager for the group
Team members discuss their work with each other, make decisions jointly, and work together toward a common goal	The manager makes decisions and allocates work among group members
Team members have individual and joint accountability for results	The manager is accountable for the group's results. Individual group members are accountable for their personal results
Performance is measured by the team's results	Performance is measured by individual results
Members are encouraged to hold open-ended discussions and participate in group problem solving	Group members either find answers themselves or ask the manager for assistance
Synergy is achieved by team members learning from each other and learning together	No synergy
The work of team members is interdependent	The work of group members is independent

Table 7-1: Differences between a Team and a Work Group

- A manufacturer of large central office telephone switches organized a group of 12 employees (who assembled one type of device) into a self-managed team. The team members worked to cross-train on various aspects of the assembly process so that they could cover for one another when someone was out sick or on vacation. They also developed their own work schedules and solved problems together. They met weekly to discuss the schedules and any new ideas for improving the workflow and productivity measures. The team members, through the cross-training, learned from one another. They also learned together how to set up schedules and to overcome bottlenecks in their assembly work.

- An automobile manufacturer put together a cross-functional team to improve the quality of one model that had a record of many major and minor defects. The team consisted of representatives from design engineering, manufacturing, services, parts, marketing, and customer-relations groups because all were involved in the design, manufacture, and service of the model or had data on problems and customer perceptions of it. The team was given a charter to examine both how to fix existing problems and how to prevent them from occurring in the next year's model. The work of team members was interdependent. For example, the engineering design would directly affect the plans and costs for manufacturing; decisions made with regard to how the car was manufactured would have consequences for how easy it would be to service; decisions on the reliability and expected lifespan of the components would have direct effects on how many spare parts needed to be manufactured and kept in inventory; and decisions on what features to add next year would be very important to the marketing of the new model. The entire team process was focused not just on having each represented function make decisions, but on the members learning how their decisions would affect all the other groups' decisions and results. This team learned from one another how decisions made in one area affected all the other areas.

- A school system appointed a team to select a new textbook to be used for teaching world history across the system's high schools. The team included teachers from the schools who would be teaching from the book, the system's social studies resource person, and a business manager. During their meetings, they not only examined new textbooks from various publishers, but also exchanged information on how they were currently teaching the world history course using the existing textbook and what they were doing in their classes to supplement the current book. Their recommendation on the new textbook also included suggestions on how the new book, and the publisher's supporting materials, should be used to revise the course's syllabus. This team learned about each new textbook together, and they learned from one another about a wide variety of instructional methods that were already being used.

- A restaurant put together a team to make recommendations on how to improve its customers' dining satisfaction, with the goal of increasing the number of return customers and improving the ratings from the city's restaurant reviewers. The team included the executive chef, kitchen staff, wait staff, and the front-of-the-house manager. Their discussions ranged from menu choices to portion sizes to prices to table settings to the uniforms for servers and bus staff. Team members learned from one another how a choice in any one of these areas affected all the others. As the recommendations for change in an area were tried, the team reviewed how those changes affected each of the other operational areas, as well as overall results. This was done in a serial manner so that the team could measure the improvements from each change. The team learned from one another how changes in one area of the restaurant's operations affected the other areas and together how their suggested changes affected the restaurant's overall results.

Barriers to Team Learning and Effectiveness

You may have worked as part of a team that was very effective or one that never seemed to accomplish much. Unfortunately, there are a number of common barriers to team effectiveness, including

- Having the wrong people on the team
- Lacking diversity of thinking styles on the team
- Seeking a personal victory rather than team success
- Suffering from groupthink
- Lacking a common vocabulary

Having the Wrong People on the Team

When a senior executive decides to put together a cross-functional team to address a problem or a challenge, he typically sends out a memo to the heads of the groups he wants to be represented, asking them to each appoint someone to serve as a member. Too often, each group manager responds by asking her staff, "Who has time for this?" rather than considering who can best represent the group and contribute to the team's work. As a result, the team ends up with members from the right groups, but quite frequently, they are not the most appropriate representatives from those groups. If your manager asks you to serve on a cross-functional team, it can be a great learning opportunity that will enable you to expand your view of the company's business, learn from other team members, build your internal network, and improve your teamwork skills. When asked to serve on such a team, you should ask your manager and yourself these questions:

- What is the purpose of the team? The team needs to have a solid charter with a well-defined purpose. Is the team empowered to make decisions, or just recommendations?
- What role does your manager want you to play? Too often, when a cross-functional team is established, the manager of each group to be represented on the team tells her group's delegate, "Your job is to go convince everyone else that our solution to the problem is the only rational choice." If every member is given this same instruction, the odds are that the team won't accomplish much. Another aspect of this question is whether you will have the authority to make commitments for your group or whether you will always need to check back with your manager: you need to know this before you start working on the team.

119

- Do you have the knowledge and skills needed to contribute to the team's work? Do you feel that you are the best person in the group to be on this team, or at least have sufficient knowledge and skills to address the team's goals competently? It is fine to stretch yourself—that's a way to learn—but it is never comfortable, and often dangerous, to be thrown into the deep end of the pool if you haven't yet learned how to swim. Of course, there are times when your role on the team may be that of the smart dummy, as discussed in Chapter 6, but you should know this before you start working in the team.

Lacking Diversity of Thinking Styles on the Team

When discussing diversity in the workforce, companies often think about ethnic, gender, and geographic diversity. While these are vital considerations, it is also important to consider diversity of thinking styles. To reach optimal results, team membership should include people with a variety of backgrounds, experiences, and thinking styles. And, as explained in Chapter 6, it is sometimes wise to include a "smart dummy" on the team to challenge the thinking of other team members.

Thomas-Kilmann Conflict Styles.

The Thomas-Kilmann Conflict Mode Instrument is often used to improve teamwork.[1] By answering a series of questions, the model measures individuals' responses on two scales: assertiveness and cooperativeness. Using these two scales, each individual is identified as having one of the following dominant conflict styles:

- *Collaborating* (high on both the assertiveness and cooperativeness scales) refers to working together with other team members to find a solution that will meet everyone's needs.
- *Competing* (high on assertiveness and low on cooperativeness) refers to working to get one's own solution selected instead of anyone else's solution.
- *Compromising* (medium on both assertiveness and cooperativeness) refers to finding middle ground—giving up some of what you want to get agreement.
- *Accommodating* (low on assertiveness and high on cooperativeness) refers to letting others have their own way.
- *Avoiding* (low on both assertiveness and cooperativeness) refers to staying out of the way of conflict situations and letting others fight their own fights without taking sides.

There is no right or wrong conflict style, but it helps to know what style each team member uses. One way of looking at diversity on teams is to take a negative example: what if all team members had the same style? If they all had a dominant style of

- *Collaborating*—the team might spend so much time ensuring that everyone's needs were met, even on the most trivial of issues, that decisions will take far too long to make.
- *Competing*—team members would spend a huge amount of time and energy fighting over every decision, with no one willing to give in.
- *Compromising*—team members might see every decision as a zero-sum game, where they will not be willing to concede any point without getting something in return.

121

- *Accommodating*—team members would quickly agree on the first idea that was offered (groupthink), whether that was the best solution or not.
- *Avoiding*—no issues would ever arise, because team members would evade them.

If you take the Thomas-Kilmann Conflict Styles Instrument, you will find that most people do not have a "pure" style, but a combination of styles. For example, my scores show me to be high on both the competing and accommodating scales, meaning that if I don't have a vested interest in an issue, I am happy to let others, who may feel strongly about it, decide (accommodating). However, if I do feel strongly about an issue, I try to sway others to my point of view (competing).

Team Composition

My first job as a manager was in a management development group in a large computer company. My group's focus was on the development of managers in the company's corporate organizations (such as manufacturing, engineering, human resources, information technology, and finance), while another manager had a group focused on field functions (such as sales and services). Our approaches to building our groups were very different. My colleague hired people who had degrees and backgrounds in instructional design. She gave each person his own project to work on, and each worked exclusively on that project. I hired a diverse group: some people with instructional design backgrounds, some with functional experience in the fields that fell under my umbrella, and others with consulting backgrounds. Each project was assigned to one person, but each project manager could rely on help from the others. My colleague had a work group, while I put together a team. While the courses her group developed were very good, I felt that my approach resulted in generally better products because of the diversity of the team members' experiences and points of view.

....

Seeking a Personal Victory rather than Team Success

Even if team members have not been mandated by their managers to sway the team to the manager's preferred solution, personal egos and the need to compete and win can stymie the success of a team. If you, as a team member, decide that the solution you are recommending is the only one that can work, you may not consider alternative solutions or even listen to others' ideas or comments. If you don't listen to others, you can't learn from them.

Perhaps your idea is the best of the lot. However, in developing your idea, you may not have considered some factors of which you were unaware. If you listen to the ideas of other team members and ask questions about how and why they developed those ideas, you will be engaging in critical thinking; if you brainstorm with other team members, you will be engaging in creative thinking, as discussed in Chapter 4. By actively engaging in these group discussions, you give yourself the best opportunity to learn, and the greatest chance for the team to arrive at the optimal solution. It may end up being your original idea, a modified version of your idea based on what you learned from team discussions, or a completely different idea from someone else or one that arose from what was learned from the discussions.

123

Suffering from Groupthink

A lot of the work of a team takes place in meetings: to planning and coordinating work, to brainstorming ideas, to finding solutions to problems. How effective the team will be can depend greatly on how well those meetings are conducted.

Groupthink occurs when members are so concerned with harmony that they accept the first idea or solution that is offered or yield to an argumentative team member's views because they don't want to create discord. While it may be more pleasant to have a totally consonant team that always reaches agreement quickly and peaceably, groupthink often leads to suboptimal results.

Teams need to put in place a set of rules for team behavior right at the beginning of the effort. One of those rules should be that team members may disagree with one another, but not be disagreeable. In Chapter 4, when discussing creative thinking, there was a short list of "idea killers"—phrases that stop ideas before they are heard. These types of comments should be banned from team conversations.

The power of a team comes from the synergy of its members and the members' ability to discuss ideas openly, to build on one another's ideas, to develop a full and common understanding of the challenges facing the team, and, together, to work toward a solution or reach a goal. If the first idea offered is always accepted without any discussion, then the team will often fail to derive the best possible solution.

Introvert versus Extravert Styles in Teams

Most teams will have some members who are introverts and others who are extraverts. One of the key differences between these two styles is that introverts typically think through an idea thoroughly before offering it to the group, while extraverts like to think as they talk. Because of this, if a team is holding a meeting to discuss ideas for solving a problem, the introverted members will offer their ideas succinctly and the extraverts will talk and talk and talk some more while developing their ideas. Introverted team members, because they have thought through what they want to say well before a meeting, may be viewed as reticent because they don't talk much; this can drive the extraverts crazy. Extraverted team members may talk seemingly endlessly because they are thinking while they talk, and their monologues may change direction several times while they are simultaneously talking and thinking. This is almost certain to frustrate the introverts.

Here are some tips for introverts:

- *When presenting an idea to the team, take some time to explain how you came to that idea, what alternatives you considered, and why you chose the idea you are presenting. This will help the extraverts on the team better understand your reasoning.*

- *Often, introverts are nervous about presenting their ideas; this is another of their basic characteristics. I am a strong introvert, and, being anxious about presenting*

125

my ideas to a team, I would often try to get my ideas stated early so that I could get it over with and relax. My problem arose when the extraverts took over and talked at length about their ideas. Often, by the time they were done talking, no one remembered my idea. Therefore, I found that if I wanted the team to consider my idea, I had to restate it briefly after the extraverts had finished.

- *When extraverts take the floor, listen to their reasoning and ask questions or make suggestions to help them think through their ideas. By asking questions, not only will you develop a better understanding of their ideas, but you will also be helping the extraverts think them through and formulate them more quickly.*

- *Because it may be difficult for you to speak up in a meeting, you need to watch out for the symptoms of groupthink. If you have a question, ask it: if you don't, you won't get an answer. In addition, if you have a better idea, or a way of improving on someone else's idea, offer it—or the team may select a suboptimal solution.*

For extraverts

- *Try to think through your ideas before a meeting so that your internal dialogue doesn't dominate. It may be helpful if you do this with another team member before the meeting—someone who can ask questions, make suggestions, and help you focus.*

- *In a meeting, listen to the ideas presented by others, as they may spark your own thinking process. If you hear an idea similar to yours, try building on it rather than starting your presentation as if the other idea hadn't been mentioned. As others are presenting their ideas, ask yourself, "Am I really listening, or am I just waiting for my turn to talk?"*

- *If an introverted team member presents an idea very succinctly, remember that he has most likely thought through the idea before presenting it. If you are not sure how he arrived at that idea, ask him to explain his thinking process, what alternatives he considered, and why he chose to present that particular idea, and do it in a way that demonstrates your willingness to learn rather than as a challenge.*

Whether you are an introvert or an extravert, team discussions can be prime learning opportunities for you and your fellow team members, so make the most of them.

Lacking a Common Vocabulary

It is important for team members to share a common vocabulary so that when a term is used, everyone understands it in the same way. If this isn't done, people may be working at cross-purposes.

Let's suppose that you are on a cross-functional team whose purpose is to design a new product and bring it to market. On the team are representatives from design engineering, manufacturing, field service, marketing, and sales. At one meeting, the question is asked: "When will we be ready to bring the product to market?" How might the phrase *ready to bring to market* be interpreted by each group?

- From engineering's point of view, the product is ready when it has been designed and has passed beta testing. At this point, engineering's work is done.

- From manufacturing's point of view, the product is ready when it comes off the manufacturing line. This means that after beta testing by engineering, manufacturing must decide how and where to manufacture the product, set up the process, order and stock the raw materials, plan the packaging for the product, and so on.

- Field service doesn't consider the product ready until they have put together a service manual for the product, ordered spare parts, and trained the field service technicians how to install and fix the product.

- Marketing may consider that their work to bring the product to market can start when the product specifications are finalized and engineering's beta testing has yielded enough data to write marketing copy about the features and benefits of the product.

- Sales reps don't want to sell the product until they know when it will be available. If the new product is a replacement for an existing product, they don't want to announce the new product too early, lest customers stop buying the existing product to wait for the new one.

As you can see, these various interpretations of a term or phrase can cause great confusion and can greatly complicate and confuse planning because each group defines the term differently, so one of the first tasks a team must undertake is to define a common vocabulary. As a team member, this can be a prime opportunity for you to learn about the perspectives of different functions within the company.

Learning from Team Experience

Many teams use after-action reviews (AARs) to improve team learning. At the completion of a project, or any major phase of a project, the team meets to answer and discuss such questions as

- What went well: how can we make certain that we get these positive results in the next project or phase?
- What didn't go well: how can we ensure that we don't make the same errors again?
- What have we learned from this project that will help us succeed with future projects?
- If we had known at the beginning of the project what we know now, what would we have done differently?

In many companies, what was learned from each AAR is shared across teams so all teams can benefit from one another's experience.

Special Considerations for Virtual and Geographically Dispersed Teams

There are some special considerations you should keep in mind when dealing with virtual or geographically dispersed teams. In these teams, members must rely heavily on communications technologies to keep in contact with one another, whether by telephone, e-mail, videoconferencing, or the various groupware tools available on the market. It is generally much easier to hold conversations and learn from one another when team members are colocated and can sit in the same room for a meeting or drop in on one another to discuss issues. It is also much easier to develop trust among team members when you are working side by side in the same location.

Two special challenges for virtual or geographically dispersed teams are

- Time barriers
- Language and cultural barriers

Time Barriers

In a team that consists of members around the globe, there can be as much as 12 hours' difference in local time. This makes it difficult to set up meetings because what is in the normal work schedule for some team members may be late evening or middle of the night hours for others. Often, the meeting schedules are set by the people in the company's central location, forcing team members in far-off countries to dial in or log in from home at very difficult hours. This can easily build resentment among those team members who are often inconvenienced. While it may be impossible to find perfect times for team meetings, you can alleviate these types of situations in several ways:

- Find times that will disrupt the remote team members' schedules the least. If most of your team is located in the United States, but you have one or a few members in Australia or the Far East, where it is 12 hours later, try scheduling your meetings early in the morning (U.S. time) so that it will be early evening in the other time zone, rather than scheduling your meetings at, say, 3:00 p.m. (U.S. time), which is the middle of the night for your remote members.

- Show some consideration for remote team members by occasionally scheduling meetings at a time that is convenient for them but not for you. With Web conference services, you can hold a meeting, for example, at 9:00 p.m. (U.S. time) so that the U.S. members of the team can participate from their homes, making it 9:00 a.m. local time for the team's most remote members.

- Use asynchronous tools, like discussion boards, to share information so that people can post their queries and retrieve their answers when it is convenient for them.

Language and Cultural Barriers

In a geographically dispersed team, there may be some members whose native language is not the same as the language used at company headquarters. If the majority of the team resides in the United States, you may find that some remote members are difficult to understand on a conference call because of their accents or because their English language skills are less than perfect. In addition, in some cultures, people are hesitant to speak up to disagree with others' ideas or to ask questions when they don't understand something that has been said. This makes it difficult for them to learn and difficult for the U.S.-based team to learn from them.

According to research by RW3 (www.rw3.com), 40 percent of geographically dispersed teams underperform, primarily because of cultural differences among members. RW3 CEO

Michael Schell has identified three steps that learning leaders can take to improve the functioning of these teams:

Part one is teams need to recognize that culture and style preferences will have an impact on the way their team behaves. People will know that philosophically, but they need to go through a cognitive recognition. Step two is to learn how culture does that. There [should be] a discussion of how culture can influence team behavior, then there's a learning process of how we do it and discussing how you do it. Step three is to define the challenges that your team then faces, because now you've given people a safe environment in which to discuss that. The key is to get a uniform, agreed-upon team operating structure—a uniform, acceptable rule book for behavior.[2]

Here are a few more ideas on how you can overcome language and cultural barriers, and facilitate individual and team learning among members.

- If at all possible, bring the entire team together at the start of the effort. Communication is always easier if members have the opportunity to get to know one another on a personal level rather than just as a voice on the phone or a name on an e-mail.
- Set up a team website where members can post progress reports, team documents, and other material related to the collective work, as well as a discussion forum where members can ask questions and get answers from others asynchronously.

- Put up a page on the team website that contains a photograph of each team member along with some basic personal information, so that team members can associate one another's name with a face when communicating by e-mail or phone. Each person's brief biography might also contain a short summary of the person's areas of expertise and experience, so that other members will know how each person on the team can act as a learning resource.

- If a team member is difficult to understand on the phone, inform that person, in advance, of the topics that will be discussed during a teleconference or Web conference meeting. Many people who have English as a second language are more comfortable and understandable when they can write their ideas and comments than when they present them orally—they have more time to consider what they are writing and aren't put on the spot for an immediate response. So ask the non-native English speakers to send their ideas, comments, and questions to another member before the meeting and have that member present the material on their behalf.

- Because some countries' cultural mores make remote team members hesitant to offer ideas, ask questions, or make suggestions, make certain that you take the time in a teleconference or Web conference to specifically ask your remote team members to contribute—and then be patient while they form their ideas and perhaps present them slowly because of language difficulties.

- If you are planning a team celebration for reaching a milestone or finding a solution to a long-standing problem or challenge, find a way of including remote team members. Be creative. For example, if company policy allows, send a bottle of champagne (or other party favors) to each remote team member, set a time for the celebration, and use videoconferencing to raise a toast together.

- If you hold regular team meetings, rotate the assignment to put together the agenda among members. This will require each member, when his turn comes, to communicate with all others to assemble the agenda. You can also ask the designated person to bring in a learning activity for her assigned meeting. Learning activities could range from circulating an article from the Web or a trade publication and leading a discussion on it to facilitating a team-building activity to presenting an overview and leading a discussion about a competitive product or service.

- Start your team teleconferences or Web conferences with a few minutes of sharing personal information, such as where you just went on vacation, how your child's soccer team is doing, or that you and your spouse just celebrated an anniversary. This type of information has little to do with the team's work, but it can be very beneficial to building relationships among team members.

In today's global business environment, virtual or geographically distributed teams are more and more common, so you need to learn how to make them effective.

Chapter Summary

A team is a group of people who have common goals and who learn from one another, or together learn something new, in order to reach those goals. Without learning, you do not have a team, but just a group of people who happen to work for the same manager. There are a number of steps that you, as a team member or team leader, should take to understand your role on the team, and how you can learn from other members while contributing to their learning. Working on a virtual or geographically dispersed team presents an additional set of challenges that should be addressed at the beginning of the collective work.

Notes

1. The Thomas-Kilmann Conflict Modes Instrument and supporting materials are available from CPP (https://www.cpp.com/products/tki/index.aspx).
2. Quoted by Agatha Gilmore in "A Distressing Virtual Reality: 40 Percent of Dispersed Teams Underperform," *Chief Learning Officer Magazine Newsletter*, June 21, 2010.

8

LEARNING ON THE WEB:
BENEFIT FROM THE GENEROSITY
OF STRANGERS

With today's connected world, you have opportunities to learn from people across the globe: people who are total strangers to you, but who are willing to share their knowledge and experiences. You can use discussion groups, affinity groups, communities of practice, and a wealth of resources on the Web to help you on your learning journey.

An Assignment in Brazil

I had been invited to give a series of workshops in Brazil and was told that they would be simultaneously translated into Portuguese. Never having worked with simultaneous translation, I posted a note on a training discussion board, describing what I would be doing and asking for any experiences or advice on working with a translator. Within a few days, I had more than 20 responses. Some were from people who had had experience working with translators, two were from translators, and others were from those who had done training with the Brazilian business community. All these people were total strangers to me, but they were all willing to share their knowledge and experience. They gave me a number of suggestions that greatly improved my Brazilian experience.

Discussion Groups on the Web

There are hundreds of thousands of discussion groups on the Web. The topics they discuss range from personal interests to family-related issues to business and professional topics. For example, groups on Yahoo.com (groups.yahoo.com) include more than 10,000 groups under the category of "financial professionals." Similarly, there are tens of thousands of groups on LinkedIn, with something for just about every personal or professional interest. As in the example above, you will probably not know more than a few of the people who subscribe to these groups, but they provide an open forum where you can ask questions, and often get answers, about topics that are of interest to you. Of course, you need to be aware that no one is screening the answers, so you should always check the replies you receive for accuracy. However, if a dozen different people give you the same answer and no one in the group is contradicting it, you can be reasonably certain that the answer is valid.

As with most of life, you should give as well as receive. If you want people in a discussion group to help you, you will have a better chance to get answers if you are also a learning resource for others. For example, I have become active in an online community called the HR (human resources) Toolbox. The managers of this community give recognition to people who contribute regularly by answering questions from others and often invite the most frequent contributors to lead one of their weekly featured discussions. Not only has this online community helped me to solve some problems and learn some new things, but it has also helped me to expand my personal learning network (PLN). (See Chapter 10 for a more complete discussion of personal learning networks.)

Communities of Practice

Communities of practice (CoP), according to leading authority Etienne Wenger, "are groups of people who share a concern or a passion for something they do and learn how to do it better as they interact regularly."[1] You can find a CoP for just about any profession, sometimes on your company's intranet, sometimes on the Internet (such as on Yahoo! Groups or LinkedIn), and sometimes on websites of professional societies or industry associations.

Wenger lists a number of ways that people can use communities of practice to help them learn:

- *Problem Solving:* "I am stuck on how to design this new product. Can we brainstorm some ideas or get some volunteers from the community to take a look at what I've done so far and make suggestions for next steps?"
- *Requests for Information:* "Where can I find a supplier for this part?" "Does someone know how to use this piece of software to do this?"

139

- *Seeking Experience:* "Has anyone run into this problem before?" "I'm trying to get an answer from this government agency, but the people I have talked with in their call center don't seem to have a clue. Does anyone know someone there who could help me?"

- *Brainstorming:* "I am writing a book on this subject. Can you suggest a good title for it?"

- *Reusing Assets:* "We have a piece of test equipment that we purchased for a specific purpose and we no longer need it. Is there some other group in the company who can make good use of it?" (Or "Is there somebody outside the company who would like to buy it?")

- *Coordination and Synergy:* "We've been buying this raw material in small quantities for use in our manufacturing process. Are there other groups in the company that use the same material? If so, perhaps we can combine our purchases and get a better price from the distributor."

- *Discussing Developments:* "Have you seen the new tax laws? Is there something we should be doing in how we account for inventory to take advantage of the new law?"

- *Documentation Projects:* "This problem seems to arise fairly often with different groups. Can we develop and document a procedure to solve the problem once and for all?"

- *Visits:* "We are really interested in the new manufacturing process you are using. Can we send some people over to learn more about it?"

- *Obtaining References:* "I want to take a course on Subject X, and I have found six alternatives: these two courses from these colleges, this course from Vendor Y, this workshop from my professional society, and this e-learning program from Vendor Z. Has anyone in the community taken any of these courses? How would you rate them?"[2]

....

A Story from Digital Equipment Corporation

When I worked at Digital Equipment Corporation in the 1980s and 1990s, the company had its own internal discussion forums (long before their emergence on the Internet) that were actually communities of practice (before that term was coined). Here's an example of how the networking discussion forum worked:

A sales rep from California posted a question on the networking discussion forum: "My customer has these IBM mainframes, these Digital computers, and these Sun workstations. They want us to network them all together. Here's the solution I am planning to propose. I'd appreciate any advice from others who have worked with similar configurations."

Within 24 hours, she had half a dozen responses, such as

- *A network specialist from New York said that the proposed solution should work, but listed a few things to watch out for.*
- *A network salesperson from the Netherlands said that he had found a third-party product that helped with a similar configuration and provided contact information for the vendor.*

> • *The regional network team in Australia said that they had developed a custom solution for a customer with a similar configuration and would be happy to discuss how they could make it available for the California customer.*
>
> *The point here is that the California sales rep personally knew none of the respondents, but all were willing to share their knowledge with her.*

....

Searching the Web to Find an Answer

Let's say that you want to learn more about a given topic. There are several ways that you can use the Web to find the information you are seeking.

- Start by putting your keywords into your favorite search engine. You will undoubtedly receive back hundreds or thousands or even millions of websites. You can start by reading through those sites that came up on the first few pages of your results to see if any of them contain the information you are looking for. Web searches can be overwhelming at times, but with practice, you can learn how to select specific key words that will narrow your results. Often this comes from looking at the first dozen or so search-engine listings, seeing which ones are most relevant to you, and then adding other terms that will focus your search more accurately.
- If you don't particularly like using a search engine for this purpose but would rather find a good book on the subject, you can go to Amazon.com or another online book dealer and use keywords to search for relevant books. A useful

feature of the listings on Amazon.com is the reader ratings and reviews of the books. You can see what others have said about each book and what they found particularly helpful or not about each one.

- There are some Web-based services that you cannot access unless you pay a membership fee. Your local library can often help with this situation. Often, libraries or professional associations pay for subscriptions to some of these online subscription services. For example, I have often used an online search service that indexes articles from hundreds of magazines and journals, and provides full-text versions for the majority of those articles right from your PC. While some of the resources they list will contain only abstracts of the articles, you can often find hard copies of those publications at your local library. My local library makes these services available to card holders from their own PCs, so you don't even have to travel to the library to use the service once you have a library card.

- Don't forget to check local college libraries as well. In doing research for the books I have written over the past 20 years, I used the library from a local college, paying them $35 per year for the privilege. Along with their online resources, they also subscribed to many of the magazines and journals that I found of interest. Also, don't underestimate the amount of help you can get from reference librarians. Their training and their jobs are to help people find the information resources they are seeking. And with interlibrary loan services, you can access hard copies of even obscure journals, even if the library you are visiting doesn't itself subscribe.

Wikipedia

Wikipedia is a free online encyclopedia developed by thousands of users around the world. The English version contains more than three-and-a-half million articles (there are millions of articles in other languages as well), all donated to the public domain by users. The uniqueness of Wikipedia is that anyone can contribute and that anyone can edit any entry. You will find some entries that are well documented and others that are not. While it contains a huge amount of useful information, you need to remember that there is no guarantee that the content is correct. Even with this warning, it can be a valuable resource for finding information and defining terms.

E-Learning on the Internet

On the Internet, there is an ever-increasing number of e-learning programs available, including

- E-learning programs created by your company for its employees that you access from your company's intranet
- Commercial e-learning courses that your company may have purchased from one or more vendors for use by its employees or that you can purchase for your own use from those same vendors
- E-learning courses (which can range from "help screens" to actual online classes) provided by vendors to help you learn how to use their products
- Distance-learning courses, for free or for a charge, that you take using the Internet, from schools, e-learning companies, professional associations, or individuals who create a

program and make it available over the Internet. Resources can carry college credit or continuing education units, often required to keep certification in some professions. (Some universities are putting free courseware on the Internet, such as MIT's Open Courseware: http://ocw.mit.edu/index.htm.)

E-learning can be a very useful tool in a number of circumstances:

- If you need to learn something and the number of employees in your company is not sufficient to justify bringing an instructor-led program in-house, e-learning may be a possible resource.
- If the people who need to learn the subject matter are scattered among many locations, e-learning eliminates travel expenses and travel time away from the job.
- When you need just-in-time learning: with e-learning, you don't have to wait until there are a sufficient number of people to justify the expense of holding a live class.
- If there is an expert, for example a college professor, who offers a course or workshop that is of interest to you, but that expert resides far away, an e-learning course given by that expert can facilitate your learning without your taking the time and travel expenses to learn at the expert's location.

E-learning can be an excellent tool when you are studying a factual subject, such as learning a new programming language or learning financial terms. For more behavioral skills, e-learning can provide some useful instruction, but it cannot match an instructor-led class where you get to practice those new skills in a safe environment. For example, if you are seeking to improve your presentation skills, an e-learning course can teach you how to structure a presentation and how to create slides for your presentation. It can show you examples of good and poor presentation skills. However, if you really want to improve your presentation abilities, you need to get up in front of a class, give a talk, and get feedback on your skills. It is also helpful if your presentation is recorded so that you can watch yourself in action and learn from your own mistakes. As discussed in Chapter 2, to get maximum value from an e-learning program, you need to focus on it in the same way that you would a classroom-based course.

Safety and Security Concerns in Using the Internet

The Internet can be a very useful resource, but it also comes with potential dangers that you should work to avoid.

- *Violating Company Policies:* When you are working on the Internet (in contrast to working on your company's intranet), you want to make certain that you are not disclosing any of your company's proprietary information. For example, in asking people how to solve a problem, you want to make certain that you are not prematurely announcing a new product or service that your business is developing or that you are not exposing a potential issue with one of your company's products that is not generally known.
- *Libel:* While you may have a strong opinion about a person, product, or company, you want to watch out that you

do not libel someone and face legal action because of it. Once something you wrote is posted on the Internet, it is very difficult to remove. A modern adage is that you don't want to post anything on the Internet (or in an e-mail) that you wouldn't want to see on the front page of the *New York Times* the next day.

- *Violating Copyrights:* While there is a lot of good information on the Internet, you may also find information that violates a person's or a company's copyrights. For example, I recently saw a listing on the Internet for a free download of one of my books from a site in Asia. I contacted my publisher to ask about this and was told that there are a number of "pirate sites" that often contain viruses that will infect your system if you try to download them. Besides the dangers of viruses, you can also face litigation if you post or use someone else's copyrighted information. There are several search engines that certify Internet sites as "safe," meaning that you won't run the risk of infecting your own system by viewing those sites.

- *Accuracy of Information:* Anyone can post almost anything on the Web. There is no service that guarantees the accuracy of posted information. For that reason, if you find an answer to a question or some useful information on the Web, you should check it with multiple Web entries to see if you get the same information. While this doesn't guarantee accuracy, if the same information is found from multiple sources, you can proceed with greater confidence.

- *Analysis Paralysis:* There is simply so much information available on the Internet that people can become addicted to it. If you do a search and get a million or more websites listed, you can't and shouldn't feel you need to check them all. As you become more familiar with your field of interest, you should start noting (in your personal learning journal, as explained in the appendix) which sites you generally find have the most useful information and check those first. If the authors of those particular sites seem to be very helpful to you, recruit them to be part of your personal learning network, as explained in Chapter 10.

Chapter Summary

The Internet can be a valuable learning resource for you. Through Internet searches, discussion boards and communities of practice (CoP), you can find a lot of useful information to meet your learning needs, and the contacts you make on the Internet and from communities of practice can help expand your personal learning network. Of course, you must watch out for a number of things when using the Internet, including violating your company's policies and other people's copyrights. However, a little bit of caution can make it a very productive tool to use in your learning journey.

Notes

1. http://www.ewenger.com/theory/communities_of_practice_intro.htm.
2. Ibid.

LEARNING FROM CONFERENCES AND TRADE SHOWS

Several years ago, I was a speaker at an e-learning conference. Just prior to the session in which I was presenting on the topic of knowledge sharing, there was an outstanding keynote speaker. At the start of my session, I asked the hundred people (mostly training managers) in my audience, "How many of you think the previous speaker had some interesting ideas that could be of value to you?" Almost everyone raised a hand. I then asked, "How many of you think that at least some of the speaker's ideas could have value for your company's CEO and other executives?" Again, almost everyone raised a hand. Finally, I asked, "How many of you plan to buy a copy of the speaker's book or a recording of his presentation and give it to your CEO?" Only two hands went up! These were training professionals: the very people whose job it is to spread knowledge in their organization!

W e do a poor job of learning from the conferences and trade shows that we attend, getting only a small percentage of the value available to us. We'll start with how you can get maximum value from attending a conference and then move on to discuss trade shows.

Why We Attend Conferences

You may attend a conference for a variety of reasons: because there are topics on the agenda that are of interest to you, to build your network of professional contacts, to learn more about new developments in your field, or to be a presenter yourself. You may also attend because you need a break from work and the conference is in a nice location and, secondarily, you might learn something useful.

When you attend a conference, you are exposed to many points of view, excellent practices, and alternative methods. You have an opportunity to ask questions of speakers, discuss ideas with other participants, and broaden your own view beyond the boundaries of your own company and, often, beyond your own industry. You can informally benchmark your own company's practices against those of other companies (represented by both the speakers and other participants).

While you can learn a lot at a conference by just listening to the presenters, you can learn even more if you actively engage the speakers and other participants in discussions about what you hear and what they are doing in their own organizations. These contacts can also serve you well in the future with respect to finding a new job, finding new talent to bring into your own organization, making contact with headhunters and consultants, and so forth. This is all part of your learning experience.

However, most people realize only a small percentage of the potential learning available from attending a conference, for them and for the companies they represent. By planning your own agenda for a conference and by asking your colleagues who won't be attending the conference if you can help them gain knowledge from the conference, you can multiply the value you receive from a conference many times.

The Costs and Benefits of Attending a Conference

When you attend a conference, you (or your company) are making a substantial investment. Costs include

- The conference registration fee
- The cost of travel and expenses
- Your salary for the days you travel to and from and attend the conference
- The opportunity costs for other activities you would be doing if you were back at the office

So, what value do you and your company get from your attendance? For most people, any knowledge acquired at the conference rarely extends beyond themselves. If the attendee shares his knowledge at all, it may be with his manager or one or two colleagues—and even then, it will typically include only one or two highlights. Overall, most attendees get very little personal value from a conference, and their companies get even less return on the investment.

Here's how you can get greater value from attending a conference.

Planning Your Conference Agenda

Most attendees don't look at the program seriously until they register in person at the start of the conference. To maximize your learning opportunities, you should review the agenda and the session descriptions at least one week before the conference. While you may not receive the full agenda beforehand, most conference sponsors keep an updated agenda on their website, so check it at least one week before the start, and print out the agenda and the session descriptions.

....

A Learning Challenge: Expand Your Horizons

Select at least one session that will be a stretch for you: a different area of expertise, a different industry perspective on a common practice, or a new area of learning that you have been thinking about but have done little toward until now.

....

Many industry and professional conferences have multiple concurrent sessions during the program, and you cannot physically attend all of them. Find out if there are others from your group or your company who will also be attending the conference, and if so, plan your agendas together so you can cover multiple concurrent sessions. By doing this, you can share your learning, as well as session handouts, ideas, and contacts, with one another.

Whether you are attending the conference alone or with a group, spend time reviewing the agenda before the conference starts. Ask yourself

152

- Which sessions appear to have the greatest potential value for me personally, for my group or team, for my function or business unit, and for the company as a whole? Set up a schedule for yourself, and for others if you are going as a group.

- How can I help my colleagues learn from the conference, even if they are not attending? If you are the only person from your work group who will be attending the conference, share the agenda with your colleagues and your manager. Ask them if there are particular sessions they would like you to attend, or at least get the handouts from. Many conferences today record sessions and sell copies; see if your colleagues want a recording of one or more sessions.

- What could I learn from the presenter that would add the most value? Write down the questions you would like to get answered in the session. (See Worksheet 9-1: Session Knowledge Worksheet)

During the Conference

Use the worksheet and questions you prepared before the conference during each session.

- Write down the answers to your questions as the speaker covers each topic.

- Add questions to your list as they arise during the presentation.

- The questions that remain unanswered at the end of each presentation will become your ready list for the question-and-answer period that typically comes at the end of each presentation.

Use this first page for preconference planning. Use Worksheet #2 to plan follow-up activities based on what you learned. Use one worksheet for each session you plan to attend.

Session Title:

Speaker:

Date/Time/Location:

What ideas in the session description are related to my work or to that of my group, department, function, business unit, or the company as a whole?

What could I learn from this session that would add the most value to my work?

Which questions do I want to make certain the speaker answers?

1.   Answer

2.   Answer

3.   Answer

4.   Answer

5.   Answer

WORKSHEET 9-1: Session Knowledge Worksheet

....

Learn by Challenging Your Own Assumptions

If a speaker's approach is very different from your own, don't immediately dismiss it. Instead, ask yourself

- *Why did the speaker choose this approach?*
- *What makes the speaker's company or situation similar to or different from your own?*
- *What if you viewed your own situation through the speaker's eyes? Could you expect a different or better result?*

....

After each session,

- If you aren't able to get answers to all your questions during the presentation or the question-and-answer time, find the speaker after the session to follow up.

- If the speaker is unavailable after the session, plan to follow up by mail, e-mail, or telephone. Most speakers put their contact information on their presentation handouts. If this speaker does not, ask the conference sponsor how to contact her.

- Use the session as a basis for discussion with other conference attendees. What have they done in their companies? How have their approaches differed from those of the speaker? What has worked for them and what hasn't?

- Make specific notes and list ideas that you want to try or discuss with others when you get back to the office.

- Even if there is nothing in a presentation that you can use yourself, think about the needs of others in your organization. Would someone else benefit from the speaker's ideas? If so, plan to share the ideas with her. Write all these ideas down on the second page of the Session Knowledge Worksheet (Worksheet 9-2); if you don't, it will be all too easy to forget them when your focus moves on to a new speaker or topic.

A Networking Tip: Finding People with Similar Interests

If the conference agenda does not include a session that exactly matches your interests or learning needs, plan your own discussion group. Ask the conference sponsor or moderator to make an announcement before lunch one day, mentioning your name and the topic in which you are interested, and to set aside a table at lunch for people who have a similar interest to sit down and discuss the issue.

A Learning Challenge: Put Ideas to Immediate Use

At the end of each session, find someone with whom you can discuss the ideas you've just heard. Perhaps the speaker is free for lunch, or perhaps you can ask someone seated near you to discuss some of the ideas during a break or over dinner. When you continue discussing the ideas from a session, you are more likely to act on them when you return to your job.

After the Conference

Your learning and networking from a conference will have value only if you use them when you return to your job. Start by reviewing all of your Session Knowledge Worksheets (a great activity for the trip home). Make two master lists (see Worksheet 9-2). On the first, list items titled "What I learned" and, for each item on this list, "How I can use this learning." On the second, list items titled "Ideas for others in the company" and, for each item, "How I will share these ideas." Then prioritize

What I Learned	How I Can Use This Learning
1.	1.
2.	2.
3.	3.
4.	4.
5.	5.
Ideas for Others in the Company	How I Will Share These Ideas
1.	1.
2.	2.
3.	3.
4.	4.
5.	5.

WORKSHEET 9-2: Session Knowledge Worksheet #2

each list. Take personal responsibility for acting on at least the top five items on each list.

Here are some ideas on how you can share your conference learning with others.

Apply Your Learning.

Perhaps you learned a new method to improve the work you are already doing. Unless the idea contradicts your organization's standard operating procedures, there is no reason why you cannot apply it immediately. If the idea affects more than just your own work, discuss the idea with your manager and colleagues first.

- You can make copies of the handouts, papers, articles, and other materials you collected at the conference and share them with the relevant people. While this is a good first step, it is not enough. You should attach a memo to the material highlighting your ideas on how the new material can best be used, what benefits you believe will accrue from adopting the new ideas, and a sketch of how you recommend adopting or adapting the ideas to your particular work situation. Follow this with a meeting to discuss the ideas, to get feedback on their potential impact, and to develop an implementation plan.
- You can prepare a presentation for your manager, your group, or others in the company, in which you summarize what you have learned, make suggestions on the benefits available from implementing the ideas, and recommend a course of action.

A Learning Challenge: Use What You Learn

A conference will have value only if you use the ideas you bring back to improve your own, your group's, or the company's performance.

Even if you can adapt an idea from the conference on your own, without having to gain support or approval from anyone else, it is often wise to put some help in place in case you run into a problem or something you don't understand as you try to implement the new approach. This support can take many forms:

- You can find another person in your group or company who attended the conference and who is interesting in trying out the new idea. Even if that person works in another part of the company, you can still provide feedback and support to each other.
- You can share your ideas with a colleague or with your manager and try to implement them together, providing feedback, coaching, and encouragement to each other.
- You can establish a personal or e-mail link with the presenter from the conference, asking if you might occasionally ask a question if a problem arises during your implementation.
- You might find other people, on the Internet or on your company's intranet, who are interested in the new approach and who can provide guidance and support to one

another. The group may include conference speakers or other conference participants with whom you established contact. There are a number of free services where you can set up a members-only discussion group for this purpose.

Sharing Ideas with Others.

Even though you might have no personal or professional use for some of the ideas that you hear at the conference, they may have value to others in your group or company. Use your Conference Knowledge Worksheets to identify those ideas and how you might share them with others. Methods of sharing those ideas include

- Sending copies of presentations and papers to people you think might find them of interest. Not only might you add value to them and their work in this way, but you will also be building your personal network within the company.
- Inviting a speaker from the conference to speak at your company.
- Arranging a site visit to a speaker's company to see how that company has implemented the ideas that you heard at the conference.
- Getting copies of a presenter's articles or books to share with others and following up with a meeting to discuss specific ideas that you think might benefit your company.
- Posting the conference materials on a real or electronic bulletin board with a note about the value you think the company could derive from the ideas. Alternatively, you could start a discussion on your company's intranet about some of the ideas.

Building and Maintaining Your Professional Network

Conferences provide great networking opportunities, but a network is valuable only if you maintain it. Have you ever returned to your hotel room at the end of a long day and emptied your pockets of a bunch of business cards—only you can't remember why you have them? Or you are emptying your briefcase one day and find a stack of business cards and don't remember where you met the people or why you have them? When you exchange business cards with someone at a conference, you should immediately write on the back of each card

- Where you met the person
- What interest(s) you share (both professional and personal)
- What/how you can learn from that person
- What/how you can help that person learn

You may never contact that person again. Or you may find that two years down the road, your position is eliminated and you would really like to contact that person whose card you have in your file—but you haven't been in touch for so long that you doubt the person will remember you. If you want to get value from your network, you need to add value to it. Here are some ways to do that:

- If you read an article or find a website that you think might be of interest to people in your network, send them a copy or a quick e-mail with the link to the article.
- If you have been contacted by a headhunter about a job in which you aren't interested, send an e-mail to people in

your network asking if they might be interested or if they know someone who would be. Not only does this keep you in the minds of people in your network, but headhunters will appreciate your help—and you might need their help in the future.

- Are you on the planning committee for a conference? Keep the people in your network in mind as potential speakers or as sources of ideas for other presentations. They will appreciate the chance to present themselves and their ideas.

- Are you traveling on business to another city? See if there is someone in your network who works in that city, and call to invite the person to dinner. Not only does this help you maintain your network, but it also gives you some interesting company for dinner, instead of ordering room service or sitting alone in the hotel dining room.

....

Build Your Personal and Professional Network

When you share new ideas with others, you build your personal and professional network, and you build your own reputation as a valuable learning resource for others, both within and outside your own company.

....

A Few More Conference Suggestions

Most conferences are planned by volunteer committees that draft agendas and recruit speakers. If you volunteer for a conference planning committee, you can benefit in a number of ways:

- You can greatly expand your personal and professional network, both with committee members and with the people you recruit to speak at the conference.
- You can ensure that the topics in which you are most interested get included in the conference agenda. You might also get to recruit some people you want to meet as speakers.
- While serving on a conference-planning committee requires a commitment of time (so you should ask your manager for permission), often the committee members are given free admission, which you can use with your manager as a trade-off for the time you need to spend working on the committee.

If, like me, you are an introvert and have difficulty introducing yourself to strangers at a conference, think about volunteering to speak at the conference. When you are a speaker on a topic that is of interest to you, you don't have to seek others out: they will come to you. And whether you are an introvert or an extravert, you can enhance your professional reputation by being a conference speaker.

Learning at Trade Shows

Trade shows, where a number of vendors have set up displays of their equipment and solutions, offer many chances for learning:

- Opportunities to learn more about your own company's products and services
- Opportunities to learn about your company's competitors

- Opportunities to learn about solutions that you can apply to your work

Many trade shows also have a schedule of seminars and workshops as an adjunct to their primary focus on vendor exhibits. Don't overlook these educational sessions. These are typically very similar to conference presentations, and you should approach them with the same preparation as for a conference as we have already discussed.

Learning More about What Your Company Offers

Your view of your company is generally limited to your own business unit or function, and you may have little knowledge of the full range of products and services that it sells to its customers. If this is your situation, spend some time at your company's exhibit to increase your knowledge. If you meet some of your company's current or potential customers at the exhibit, ask them about their situations and how they are using, or considering using, the products or services—the views of current and potential customers about your business can be quite different from the views from inside the company.

....

A Learning Challenge: Volunteer to Work in Your Company's Booth

Many companies look for employee volunteers to work in the company's exhibit or booth at trade shows. When they get these volunteers, they train them not just on how to interact with visitors to the booth, but also on the full range of products and services that will be displayed in the exhibit. If your regular job is in a support function that is not directly related to the company's products and services, this is a great opportunity to expand your views and knowledge about your company.

Learning about Your Company's Competitors

Attending a trade show is an excellent way to see what products and services your company's competitors are offering to their customers, so spend some time in their booths. How do their products and services compare to your company's similar offerings? What are they saying to their current and potential customers about your company? Look at the badges of visitors to your competitors' exhibits to see what kinds of organizations are interested in their offerings compared with those who visit your company's exhibit. If you can, start a conversation with a few of the visitors to your competitors' exhibits and ask them how they view your company in comparison with your competitors. (This has to be done subtly because your competitors will not look kindly on representatives of your company talking with their customers in their exhibits.)

Learning about Solutions You Can Use in Your Work.

If you are attending a trade show for your profession, as contrasted to one for your industry, you will see a great many vendors who are displaying their products and services related to your profession. Visit their exhibits and learn all you can about what they have to offer. You may learn about new applications, new products, and new services that might be of value to you and your group. Keep an open mind—just because your company or your group has been using one vendor's product for years doesn't necessarily mean that it is the best product on the market, and new vendors can spring up suddenly who may have an even better product that would benefit your work. Collect the relevant literature and business cards, and discuss what you saw with your manager and your colleagues when you return to your job.

You should also engage other visitors to the various vendors in conversation to find out what products they are using, how they are using them, and how happy or displeased they are with those products. View this as doing some informal benchmarking. If you hear about a great success from an exhibitor or another trade show attendee, get the contact information and see if it would be possible to visit the vendor or one of the vendor's customers to see what they are doing and make your own judgment about the applicability to your own situation.

You Are Your Company's Representative

It doesn't matter what your job is or at what level of management you work—when another person sees your company name on your badge, you represent your company to that person, so you should be the best representative of the company that you can be.

- If someone asks you about your company's products or services, and you have no personal knowledge to share, don't brush the person off. If your company is exhibiting at the conference or trade show, offer to escort the person to your company's booth and introduce the person to someone who will know or be able to get the answer. If your company is not exhibiting, ask for the person's business card and write the question on the back of the card. When you get back to your office, find the right person to answer the question and ask him to call your contact. If you aren't sure who the right person is, ask your manager for help in identifying him or her.

- If someone complains to you about one of your company's products or services, again get the person's business card and write the complaint on the back. When you return to the office, get the complaint to the right person: someone who can resolve the situation. Again, ask for your manager's help if you are uncertain where you should direct the complaint.

Chapter Summary

Attending industry and professional conferences and trade shows offers you many opportunities to learn from session speakers and fellow attendees, as well as to build your professional network. In order to get maximum benefit from these types of events, you should develop a learning plan well before the event and follow up on that plan throughout and after the event. These types of events also provide opportunities for you to help your colleagues who will not be attending also learn by sharing with them.

BUILDING YOUR PERSONAL
LEARNING NETWORK

Learning doesn't take place just in training programs; it should be part of every employee's daily activities. You learn every time you read a book or article, every time you observe how someone else is doing work similar to your own, every time you ask a question. An important part of learning is to build your own personal learning network: a group of people who can guide your learning, point you to learning opportunities, answer your questions, and give you the benefit of their own knowledge and experience, as well as point you to additional learning resources in their own networks.

We started Chapter 1 with a model of the Four Stages of Learning. Let's go back to it (see Figure 10-1) to review how people learn and then discuss how developing a personal learning network (PLN) can help you learn.

In today's business world, we are all inundated with data (Stage 1): all those manuals, brochures, memos, letters, reports,

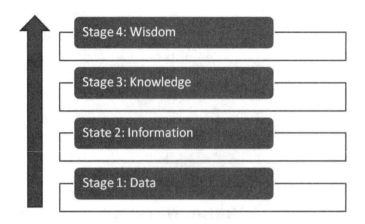

FIGURE 10-1: The Four Stages of Learning

and other printed material that cross our field of vision every day, not to mention all the e-mails, Web pages, and other materials we see electronically. I once researched how much data salespeople in a large computer company received. The average salesperson received a stack of mail almost two feet high every month. There is no way that the salesperson could even look through all of it, never mind actually read and learn from it.

When you sift through all the data you receive and identify that which is most relevant and purposeful for your work, you create information (Stage 2). Information is the minimum requirement for your learning activities. However, even when you have information, you must use it by applying it to your work before you can say you "know it." Until you use it, it remains information. Knowledge (Stage 3) comes from applying information to your work.

Wisdom (Stage 4), that most precious possession, comes from adding intuition and experience to knowledge. For example, in a paper mill, an operator may know that the mixture of chemicals in a vat is correct by the way the static electricity from that vat affects his hair as he walks by. This learning can come only from experience: it cannot be taught in a classroom or explained in a textbook, but must be personally demonstrated if it is to be transmitted from one person to another.

Using this model, we can identify the challenges you face when you want to learn something new. First, you must sort through all the available data to find what is most relevant and purposeful for your work. Then, after you have gathered and learned this information, you need to apply it to your work in order to transform it into your personal knowledge.

Why You Need a Personal Learning Network

Given the wide proliferation of information on the Internet and from other sources, you sometimes need a guide to sort through it all and more easily find what is important. If you do a Google search on any given topic, you will likely get back thousands, if not a million or more, references. The people in your personal learning network (PLN) who have background and experience in the subject you wish to learn can help you navigate through this maze of information and point you to the best learning resources they know.

Another of the problems inherent in learning something new is that while you are learning it (such as in a classroom; from reading a book, article, or Web page; or taking an e-learning course), you often don't know what questions to ask. If this is a new area of learning that you have never experienced, you may think that you understand the information, but you really won't know if you have mastered it until you try to apply it to your work. However, when you try to apply it and a question arises, there may not be anyone available to address your question. The instructor of a training program is probably off training other people. The creator of the e-learning course may not be known to you. The author of the book, article, or Web page you read is a stranger to you. Unless your manager or a colleague is a subject-matter expert on the topic, you are stuck with the question, with no one to supply an answer.

So, too often, when you face a problem with the new methods, you revert back to your old ways of getting the job done. They may not be as effective or as efficient as the new methods that you recently learned, but you know they work and you know how to use them. This is why having a PLN is so important— not only to provide you with pointers to sources of information, but also to answer your questions, to coach you, and to reinforce your learning as you try to apply it to your work. This can help you turn it into your personal knowledge. The resource people can often act as a sounding board for your ideas.

Who Should Be Included in Your Personal Learning Network

The members of your network should start with your manager and your colleagues, but members do not need to be people with whom you work directly. In fact, you do not even need to know the people personally. The members should be people, both inside and outside your work group and your company, who have the knowledge that you are trying to master and who are willing to share their knowledge and experience with you.

Let's put them in the following categories (see Figure 10-2):

- Your current and past managers
- Your current and former colleagues
- Mentors and coaches
- Members of relevant professional societies
- People you have met at conferences or trade shows
- People in online communities of practice
- Professors, trainers, authors, and other subject-matter experts
- People in your social networks

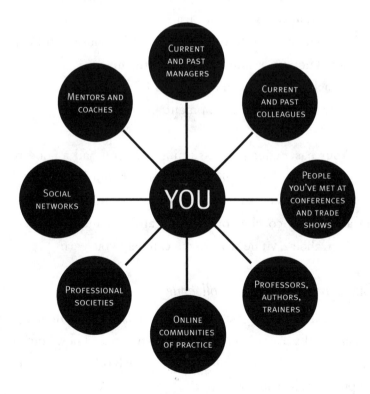

FIGURE 10-2: Your Personal Learning Network

Your Current and Past Managers

You should view your current manager as your key learning partner and resource. Your manager can help you learn in many ways, including

- Giving you feedback on your job performance and identifying your learning needs
- Providing on-the-job training
- Answering your questions
- Sending you to internal and external training programs
- Introducing you to other people and resources in the company that can assist your learning
- Introducing you to other people and resources in his personal networks external to the company
- Coaching you as you apply your learning to your work
- Advising you on development and career paths

Your past managers, assuming that you had a good relationship with them, should also be part of your PLN. Whether they are in your current company or at a former employer, they can also act as coaches or mentors and can introduce you to people in their own networks who can help you learn.

Your Current and Past Colleagues

Your personal learning network should include current and past colleagues. Every person has a different set of knowledge and experiences, and by sharing these with each other, every person is a potential learning resource.

- If you are new to a job and don't understand the local jargon or see acronyms whose meaning you don't know, a colleague who has been in the company for a while can certainly explain them to you.
- If you encounter a problem situation in your work and don't know how to solve that problem, perhaps a colleague has run into a similar problem and found a way to resolve it.
- Your colleagues have their own networks and may be able to introduce you to someone who can help you meet your learning need.
- If you have an idea for improving your own or your group's work methods, you can bounce ideas off your colleagues to develop them further before taking them to your manager.
- Your colleagues may know of books, articles, and other learning resources that could help you.

Mentors and Coaches

If your company has a formal mentoring program and you can enroll in it, your mentor can be a valuable learning resource. A mentor's role is to help you, the mentee, learn about the company's culture, provide a sounding board for ideas, make suggestions for your personal learning and development, and provide career guidance. Some companies provide mentors to all new college hires, while others restrict participation to employees who have been designated as having high potential for future leadership roles. You should check with your company's human resources department to find out if your company has a formal mentoring program and, if so, how you can qualify for it.

175

If your company does not have a formal mentoring program, you can also try to find your own mentor. Your mentor can be someone in the company or outside the company—perhaps someone you once worked for elsewhere or someone you met at a conference. There are a number of good books on how to find a mentor as well as the respective roles of mentor and mentee, and you'll find some suggestions in the bibliography at the end of this book.

While the role of the mentor is very broad, the role of a coach is very specific. The mentoring relationship can last for one or more years, while a coaching relationship will last for as long as it takes you to learn something new or master a new skill or behavior. A coach typically helps you improve your performance in one area of your work. It is important that a coach have opportunities to see you in action, so a coach should be someone in your current workplace. You can ask your manager or a colleague to be your coach, or you can find another person in the company who is already an expert in the subject matter you want to learn. It is not uncommon, for example, for a manager to assign a current employee to coach a new employee during the first few weeks on the job.

Many companies view the hiring of an external coach as expensive, and therefore use external coaches only in very specific situations, often as a final effort to save a senior executive who is failing in his or her job. The challenges in getting an external coach are, first, that an external coach will have fewer opportunities to see you in action and, second, that he may want to be paid by the company or you for his time, although many people are willing to coach another person in their PLN on a short-term basis free. However, you will never know if someone in your PLN is willing to act as your coach on a specific topic unless you ask.

As you meet people in your work, you should take note of their areas of expertise so that you may ask them to coach you if the need arises.

Professional Societies

There are thousands of professional societies in existence, some focused on specific professions (e.g., the American Medical Association, the American Bar Association), others on a more general category of jobs (e.g., the Society of Manufacturing Engineers, the Institute of Electrical and Electronics Engineers, the American Institute of Certified Professional Accountants), and others on specific industries (the Society of American Manufacturers, the Biscuit and Cracker Manufacturers Association). Most have websites, offer educational programs, and run annual conferences and trade shows. Many have local chapters that provide opportunities for you to meet people in your profession or industry from different companies, feature speakers at monthly meetings, and sometimes run local educational programs.

Attending programs at the local, regional, and national levels put on by these associations offers you opportunities to learn and to build your personal learning network. Getting to know the membership will help you identify people who have learning interests similar to your own, as well as subject-matter experts who can provide instruction, point you to learning resources, or coach you.

You can expand your personal learning network by joining the local association chapter or, even better, becoming active in the local association. Becoming an active member of an association enables you to meet more members as well as plan educational programs and conferences and have influence on their content.

People You Meet at Conferences and Trade Shows

In Chapter 9, you learned how to get the most value from conferences and trade shows. Think about the contacts you make at these events. Who has expertise in a subject you want to learn? Who has learning interests similar to your own? Who has taken an approach different from your own that you would like to explore? Who works for another company where you would like to benchmark an innovative process? From speakers to exhibitors to fellow participants, all are candidates to become part of your personal learning network.

Online Communities of Practice

No matter what your job, somewhere there is a community of practice that you can join and learn from. The Business Dictionary defines a community of practice as an "Informal, self-organized, network of peers with diverse skills and experience in an area of practice or profession. Such groups are held together by the members' desire to help others (by sharing information) and the need to advance their own knowledge (by learning from others)." You may find a community of practice related to your job in any of these places:

- Your company's intranet may include discussion areas for many aspects of your company's business.

178

- Professional associations often have online communities of practice set up for many specialties within the broader profession.

- Business networking sites, such as LinkedIn, have thousands of groups related to virtually every profession. Within those groups, members hold discussions, asking questions and answering questions from others. If you don't find a group related to your interests, you can always start one and see who else has similar interests or subject-matter expertise.

Professors, Authors, and Trainers

Does your job relate to what you studied in college? If so, some of your former professors probably have subject-matter expertise related to your work and may be willing to continue helping you learn long after you have graduated. And if your learning need is not related to their specialty, professors have their own networks and may be able to refer you to someone else for assistance.

Did you read a book or article related to your work that piqued your learning curiosity? Conduct an Internet search on the name of the author. Many authors have websites that either list their e-mail address or have a way for you to leave a message for the author. Many authors are willing to take some time to answer questions from readers, although some will insist that you hire them as a consultant if you want to pick their brains.

If an article that catches your attention is in a professional journal, you can try the same process as with a book author. If the article is written by a magazine writer rather than a subject-matter expert, the writer usually will have interviewed a number of subject-matter experts and may be able to provide you with introductions to those people to help you get more information.

When you take a training program, the trainer is a good candidate for your personal learning network and should be willing to follow up with you on any questions you have as you start applying the program content to your work. If the training is provided via e-learning, you may not have an instructor to contact, but perhaps the e-learning vendor can tell you which subject-matter experts provided the program content.

Your Social Networks

With the vast popularity of social networking tools, such as My-Life, Facebook, and Twitter, many people, especially those in Generation Y and Millennials, have vast social networks, sometimes including hundreds or a thousand or more contacts. You should sort through all your contacts, separate out those who are most relevant to your learning needs, and include them in your PLN.

How to Use Your Personal Learning Network

My CEO called me into his office. He had just read an article about scenario planning and wanted to learn more. Could I find some good reading materials for him and his direct reports, and get someone to provide training for the executive staff on this technique? Of course I could, but I would have to learn more.

I read a copy of the article that had captured his interest. I did a search on "scenario planning" on the Internet and found additional background material as well as a few business schools and consultants who offered training on the technique. I read the additional material and contacted the training providers to get information on what they taught, how much it cost, and some references from companies where they had given their seminars. I also knew that there were a few people in my network, chief learning officers at other companies, who had sponsored training on scenario planning in their organizations. I called them and asked about their experiences with the trainers they had used.

Within a couple of days, I was able to provide the CEO and his executive staff with some reading materials for background and to give him my recommendations for bringing in a training program for the executive staff. And, having used my learning network to check out a number of trainers, I was able to confidently recommend a consultant to do the training.

You use your PLN to benefit from the knowledge and experience of its members. When you have the right people in your network, they can help you in many ways by

- Pointing you to learning resources, including books, websites, articles, training programs, and so forth
- Pointing you to expert individuals who can help you solve a problem or coach you when you hit a stumbling block

- Coaching you in a new area of learning
- Sharing their experience with you
- Warning you about potential traps, roadblocks, and other obstacles you may encounter as you try to implement what you are learning
- Sharing contacts with people in their personal learning networks when they cannot help you directly
- Acting as a sounding board for you, and helping you to develop your ideas further

Maintaining Your Personal Learning Network

Each member has a different set of education, expertise, and experience, and you should keep track of what areas of interest you share so that you can focus your questions and requests for assistance on specific people. You should spread your inquiries among the members of your PLN so that you don't overburden any one person. Also, find out how each of your members prefers to be contacted—you may love to tweet, but if your contacts don't use Twitter, they may not get your messages;—you need to use the communication method that each member prefers.

Be patient with your members. Remember that they all have their own jobs to do and that they are helping you as a favor to you, not because they owe you anything. If you send someone a request, you may not hear back from him immediately—or at all. It may be that he is too busy with his own work or that he doesn't have an answer and doesn't know others who could help you. Don't nag!

Be a Resource as Well as a Requester

A PLN is a two-way street. While you may view it as a resource to help you in your work, you also must ensure that the relationship is reciprocal—that you give as well as receive. Here are some ways that you can maintain your PLN:

- If you read an article or find a website of particular interest, think about which members of your PLN might also find it interesting and valuable. Send those members a copy of the article or a link to the website along with a short note or e-mail about why you thought they might find it of interest.

- Let people in your PLN know if you are going to be attending a conference or trade show and see if they also plan to attend. If you are presenting, invite them to attend your presentation. If they are presenting, attend their presentation and say hello afterwards. Otherwise, ask them to lunch or dinner during the event: personal contact can be very important in building the relationship.

- Let them know what you are doing, the kinds of projects on which you are working, new ideas you are trying out, and so forth, and show interest in their work as well.

- Be a resource for them: answer their questions if you can, or, if you don't have an answer, refer them to someone else in your PLN who might be able to help them.

- If you receive a call from a headhunter about an open search, refer the job to anyone in your PLN that you may think might be interested in it. If you don't know anyone who might be interested, help the headhunter network with members of your PLN. The headhunter will remember you as a valuable resource, which can help you if you need to find a new job in the future, and your PLN contacts will be grateful for helping them land a new position for themselves or for others in their networks.

- If you are traveling on business to a city where someone in your PLN resides, invite him or her to meet you for a meal or for a drink or coffee to build your personal relationship.

Use—But Don't Become Totally Dependent on—Your Personal Learning Network

A final cautionary note: don't become too dependent on your PLN. You need to develop your own knowledge and skills and become self-reliant to the extent that you can do your own job well—not perfectly, but well. If you keep looking for the "perfect" answer to every problem you face, you will never get anything done. And if you keep sending requests to your PLN, people may feel that they are doing your job for you and drop out of the network.

Chapter Summary

Building a personal learning network can help you to expand your knowledge and skills by learning from others. Members of your network can include current and past managers and colleagues; people you have met at conferences, trade shows, and professional societies; people from communities of practice that you join; and people in your social networks. You need to get to know each person in your network so that you can funnel the right requests for information to the right people. In order to maintain your network, you need to keep in touch with people and offer your own knowledge, skills, and experience as resources for them.

APPENDIX

YOUR PERSONAL LEARNING JOURNAL

Throughout this book, as we have examined a variety of learning methods you can use in your everyday work, we have suggested that you keep track of your learning by keeping a personal learning journal. What is a learning journal? It is a way for you to keep a log of your ideas and reactions, what you have learned and what you want to learn, the results of your experiments, and future experiments you would like to try. It includes questions you have had and answers you have found; what you have gleaned about yourself and about others; insights about your values, biases, and personal preferences; observations of the management and leadership styles of others; and connections you have made between new learning and past learning—those "Aha!" moments when everything seems to fall into place.

Remember that this is a *personal* journal. It need not be shared with anyone. Choose the method that you find easiest to use: you can use a notebook to keep track of things or keep your journal as a file on your personal computer.

Here are some specific ideas for the types of entries you might make in your journal, but don't limit yourself to just these ideas: put in anything you feel will help you in your learning and career journey.

- In talking with others, in listening to presentations at staff meetings, in reading training or other materials, and so forth, if there are terms or acronyms that you don't recognize or about whose meaning you are unclear, write them in your journal as things to learn.

- In attending a class or taking an e-learning course, if there are topics that you don't understand fully, write down your questions in your learning journal. You can then ask your questions in the class, ask the instructor during a break, ask a classmate for help, ask your manager for clarification, or ask a friend or colleague to help you with the answer.

- It is rare for a person to attend a training program or take an e-learning course and feel that every bit of material was relevant to his situation. At the end of each formal learning experience, write down the few main ideas that you feel are most pertinent to your situation and your work, and what you want to do with each one.

- If you are reading an article or book or listening to a presentation and an idea strikes you as something that could help in your or your group's work, make a note to follow up by discussing it with colleagues or with your manager. Similarly, if an idea strikes you as something that could be helpful to someone you know, to another group with which you are familiar, or to the company as a whole, write it down as something to share with that person or group. Remember that if you help others learn, they are more likely to be willing to help you learn as well.

- From your reading, conversations, or other sources, write down any points that you found especially interesting and about which you would like to know more.

- After you have taken an e-learning class, write down the three or four main points you got from the class. Do this right after the class and before reviewing your notes. Then compare what you remembered with your notes to see if you got them right.

- Sometimes, when you take a class, read a book or article, or participate in a discussion, an idea will start forming in your head. Even if it is not fully developed yet, write the idea down in your journal so that you can refer back to it and refine it later.

- People will sometimes wake up in the middle of the night with an idea, something their subconscious has been working on while they sleep. If this happens to you, write it down. Otherwise, you may not remember it when you get up in the morning.

- When you attended a conference or trade show, was there a speaker or a person you met that you would like to add to your personal learning network? Was there a product you saw about which you would like to learn more? Did a speaker have an article or book you'd like to read?

- In observing how your manager or other managers run meetings, coach employees, manage performance, and set goals, are there behaviors that you would like to emulate when you get to that level? Are there behaviors they display that you want to be certain to avoid? ("When I become a manager, I'm never going to do that to my people!")

- When working as part of a team, observe the behaviors of team members and the leader. What seems to work well that would you like to emulate? What seems to work poorly that you want to avoid? What lessons did you learn from the after-action review (as discussed in Chapter 7) that you want to make certain you do in future projects? You can also do your own after-action reviews for your own work and make notes about how you want to do things the same way or differently in the future.

- When surfing the Internet to find information, are there some sites that seem to be full of relevant knowledge and wisdom? Write them in your journal (and bookmark them on your Web browser).

Reflection

Going back to the model of the Four Stages of Learning in Chapter 1, remember that wisdom is developed from dialogue, demonstration, experience, intuition, and experimentation. However, to truly develop wisdom, you have to reflect upon what you have learned from experience and these other learning methods, and you need to set aside time for reflection. One of the true faults with today's connected world is that you can be so tied up with e-mails, text messages, tweets, phone calls, and other distractions that constantly interrupt your day that you don't have time for reflection. To be a truly effective learner, you need to take some time every week, if not every day, to shut out these distractions and reflect on what you have absorbed and what you need to learn.

Try to focus some of your entries in your journal by reflecting on such questions as

- What have you learned about yourself and your emotional responses to learning?
- What have you learned that relates to you, your work, and your colleagues?
- What have you learned about yourself that will help you decide on your desired career path?
- What part of the learning was hardest for you? What part was easiest?
- What surprised you the most from what you learned?
- What "Aha!" moments did you have?
- What have you learned about your personal preferences in the way you learn? In the way you work? In the way you relate to your manager? In the way you relate to colleagues?
- Was there something in what you learned that evoked a strong emotional response (positive or negative) in you? Why do you think your response was so strong?
- If something confused you, what is the best way to settle the confusion?
- Was there someone in your class, meeting, or conversation that you would like to include in your personal learning network?

Keeping and Using Your Personal Learning Journal

You should use a notebook for your personal learning journal. It can be the same type you use to keep track of meeting notes and work notes, or it can be a blank book journal. Make it a different size or color from the notebooks you normally use in your work so that it will be easy to find and remember.

Try carrying your learning journal with you. If you find this inconvenient, make your learning notes in your regular notebook and circle them in red, or find some other way of distinguishing your learning notes from other writing. Then transfer them to your learning journal as soon as you can. Keep a pad and pen on your bedside table to record those ideas or insights you have while you are sleeping, write them down when you wake up in the middle of the night or in the morning, and transfer them to your journal.

You should be making notes in your learning journal almost every day. You can organize your journal into sections, such as terms and acronyms to be defined, learning from formal training, learning from after-action reviews, and lessons learned from errors, or you can just let it flow freely. If you find you have nothing to write in the journal for a week or more, ask yourself why you aren't learning—if you are not learning on a regular basis, you are doing little to improve your job performance or advance your career.

You should also take some time every week to review what you have written in your learning journal. Many ideas, whether personal brainstorms or references to an article or a term to be defined, will vanish quickly from your consciousness if you don't act on them immediately. By reviewing what you have written, you can remind yourself of what you had intended to do. Once you have completed your review, set a learning agenda for the coming week: What questions need answering? What should you be reading? What new methods do you want to try?

You have many opportunities to learn every day as part of your job. By keeping a personal learning journal, you can keep track of your learning, plan your personal learning agenda, and make yourself more aware, both of what you have learned and of your opportunities to learn.

What did you learn at work today?

Bibliography

The following are some books where you can learn more about some of the topics discussed in this work.

Adams, Marilee, *Change Your Questions, Change Your Life* (Berrett-Koehler, 2009).

Brassard, Michael, et al., *The Memory Jogger II: A Desktop Guide of Tools for Continuous Improvement and Effective Planning* (Goal QPC, 2004).

Brookfield, Stephen D., *Developing Critical Thinkers* (Jossey-Bass, 1991).

DeBono, Edward, *Serious Creativity: Using the Power of Lateral Thinking to Create New Ideas* (HarperBusiness, 1993).

Galindo, Javy, *The Power of Thinking Differently* (Hyena Press, 2009).

Glickman, Rosalene, *Optimal Thinking* (Wiley, 2002).

Hock, Randolph, *The Extreme Searcher's Internet Handbook* (third edition), (Information Today, Inc., 2010).

Katzenbach, Jon, and Douglas Smith, *The Wisdom of Teams* (Harper, 2003).

Lencioni, Patrick, *The Five Dysfunctions of a Team* (Jossey-Bass, 2002).

Martin, Chuck, et al., *SMARTS: Are We Hardwired for Success?* (AMACOM, 2007).

Pink, Daniel, *A Whole New Mind: Why Right-Brainers Will Rule the Future* (Riverhead Trade, 2006).

Tobin, Daniel R., and Margaret Pettingell, *The AMA Guide to Management Development* (AMACOM, 2008).

Wenger, Etienne, et al., *Cultivating Communities of Practice* (Harvard Business Press, 2002).

Zachary, Lois, and Lory Fischler, *The Mentee's Guide: Making Mentoring Work for You* (Jossey-Bass, 2009).

Index

About the Author

Daniel Tobin is a consultant on corporate learning strategies and leadership development programs, and a coach to corporate training directors.

With more than 30 years of experience in the learning and development field, he has founded two corporate universities and served as vice president of design and development at the American Management Association. He has given keynote speeches and workshops on five continents and written seven books on corporate learning strategies.

Tobin earned a master's degree from the Johnson Graduate School of Management and a Ph.D. in the economics of education, both from Cornell University.

Daniel Tobin can be reached at danieltobin@att.net. You can also check out his website for this book at www.whatdid youlearnatworktoday.com.